Eyes That Speak

Who's on the cover?

President Donald Trump	Aretha Franklin	Robert Meuller	Angelina Jolie
Robert DeNiro	**Eyes That Speak**		George Clooney
Supreme Court Justice Brett Kavanaugh	CHRISTY BOWE		The Dalai Lama
Bruce Springsteen	President Barack Obama	Ellen DeGeneres	Supreme Court Justice Ruth Bader Ginsberg
President Bill Clinton	Mother Teresa	Muhammad Ali	Oprah Winfrey
President George W. Bush	Princess Diana	Roger Daltrey	Secretary of State Hillary Clinton

Eyes That Speak

One Woman News Photographer's

Journey With History Makers

CHRISTY BOWE

*I dedicate this book to my parents, Patricia and Donald Bowe,
who were my cub reporters and always believed in me,
my potential and this undertaking.*

Eyes That Speak: One Woman News Photographer's Journey With History Makers

Copyright © 2021 by SheaDean Publishing LLC

All rights reserved. No part of this book may be reproduced or transmitted in any form or by any means, electronic or mechanical, including photocopying, recording, or any information storage and retrieval system, without permission in writing from the author.

ISBN: 978-0-578-30039-9

Library of Congress Control Number: 2021919926

Printed in the United States of America   1 0 0 5 2 1

∞ This paper meets the requirements of ANSI/NISO Z39.48-1992 (Permanence of Paper)

All photos property of Christy Bowe and ImageCatcher News unless otherwise indicated.
Pictures in this book may be purchased for personal use only at **www.imagecatchernews.com**

Acknowledgments

Every author owes a debt of gratitude. My first thanks go to my sister and brother,
Cathy and Donnie Bowe, for their encouragement. The late Sarah McClendon: I thank you for giving me a chance. I also appreciate my friend Warren Bowes' loyal friendship and help in countless ways over the years, both in helping with this book and the adventures in my life.

The original catalyst for this book was my good friend, the late Gerry Sparks.
Recognition belongs to all those who have helped me get to the finish line with this book:
Father Jim Meyers and Ruth Dalton — my core editing crew — have been on board with this project since the start and have contributed countless hours of vital feedback and support.
I give special thanks to Priscilla Blackburn, my first responder and friend, for coming through for me once again. Meg Crisler, Doug Otto, Catherine Whit, I appreciate all your input.

My cheerleaders who nurtured my spirit and kept me going for over a decade while working on this book are Susie Kernan, Susan Bruning, Barbara Bryniarski, Nadine Otto, Bette Crockett, the late Isabel Crockett, Andrea and Steve Kohn, Chris Sorge, Dan Straub, Peggy Burke, Steven Tammsaar, the staff at BookLogix and SheaDean Publishing, Jean Sady, Joe and Maureen Dalton, Marcie Katcher, Karen Preysnar, Betty Fraser, Laurie Meadows, Lorna Triplett of the Copyright Office at the Library of Congress and my friends and neighbors in Bethesda-Chevy Chase, MD, and the Gardens of Ocean City, NJ. I thank each of you for your interest and encouragement. The late sister Beth Dowd, O.S.U., thank you for having seen something in me long ago.

I would like to express appreciation to the photographers and reporters who are
friends and colleagues that have shown support in various ways over the years:
Greg Mathieson, Ron Sachs, Mark Reinstein, Marty vanDuyne, John Gizzi, Patsy Lynch and the late Harry Hamburg.
To those photographers who have been in the middle of a scrum with me and may have been
at the receiving end of my elbows, I say, "Sorry ... it was only business."

The U.S. Senate Press Photographers' Gallery staff: Jeff Kent, Mark Abraham, Tricia Munro and Matt Grant,
who continue to make life civilized for all of us. I also greatly appreciate the staff
of the National Press Club and members of the Photo Committee.

A very special shout-out to Kevin Lewis, a former White House staffer that came to my rescue when
he gave me a personal escort to a very hectic and overcrowded preset at a Presidential Medal of Freedom ceremony
in the East Room while I was on a walker recovering from knee surgery.

Members of my tech team added invaluable services: Mark Scoble, Doug Bolst, Seth Kaplan,
Caroline Coppel, proofreader and fact checker; Jim Dunn at Big Fat Cat; layout designer Maire McArdle
of Square House Studio.

And finally, I am grateful to God for the opportunities I have been given and the experiences I have witnessed over these years. My camera has been a unique passport to capture history as it has unfolded before my eyes.

Contents

	Foreword	8
Chapter 1	She Who Would Not Be Ignored	9
Chapter 2	My Shooting Style	13
Chapter 3	President William Jefferson Clinton	21
Chapter 4	Growing Proud and Humble	33
Chapter 5	Indebted to a Dynasty Icon	35
Chapter 6	Rendezvous With Royalty	39
Chapter 7	Innocent Infiltrator	43
Chapter 8	Peace on Earth	45
Chapter 9	President George W. Bush	49
Chapter 10	Diamonds, White Ties and Tiaras	65
Chapter 11	From Prisoner to President	71
Chapter 12	An Encounter With James Bond	73
Chapter 13	My Three Presidents	75
Chapter 14	Shaking Hands With Cool Hand Luke	77
Chapter 15	Presidents, Protocol and Pageantry	79
Chapter 16	Mother Teresa	93
Chapter 17	One More for "The Gipper"	95
Chapter 18	Hijinx With Holiness	101
Chapter 19	Old-World Charm	113
Chapter 20	President Barack Obama	115
Chapter 21	Lest Ye Be Judged	127
Chapter 22	Dustup at the China State Arrival	139
Chapter 23	The Rich, Famous and Just Plain Cool	141
Chapter 24	President Donald J. Trump	153
Chapter 25	Insurrection	185
Chapter 26	President Joseph R. Biden	195
	Author's Biography	201

Foreword

IF YOU WANT TO KNOW what is going on at the White House, ask the photographers who regularly position themselves by the barricades at 1600 Pennsylvania Ave. Photographers are the best reporters I know. Christy Bowe is an intrepid White House photographer who has covered three administrations starting with our 42nd president, William Jefferson Clinton. She has written a fascinating book: *Eyes That Speak*, a photographic documentary of American leaders in recent decades.

Bowe covers much of the Washington scene and its history-making events, but the centerpiece of her book is the White House political landscape with its steady parade of world leaders. She is among the select corps of skilled news photographers and runs her own ImageCatcher News Service. Washington photographers are the true witnesses to presidential history, and they don't have a second to lose in the competition for a great picture. The cameramen and women see the tiny bandage on a president's nose, the new hearing aid in his ear, the fleeting frown in irritation and the forced presidential bonhomie when they realize their presence is barely tolerated by a president and his staff but who, nevertheless, want their pictures to land on front pages. Still, White House photographers know nothing can replace being there.

Their so-called photo ops are planned and controlled to show the president at his best and most powerful. But sometimes a cameraman has captured an expression that was impromptu and unexpected, and that is the picture a photographer is looking for. Bowe, a regular White House photographer, managed to stage her own widely published exclusive photograph when she talked three presidents — Carter, Clinton and Ford — into posing together at a Truman Library fundraiser. She is one of the few females in the rarified press pools who go into the Oval Office for picture-taking. Christy comes from a third generation of Washingtonians. She was thrown out of Catholic School for rebelling against the nuns who did not appreciate her free spirit. As she was ousted from the ninth grade, she found her niche in a man's world with that same spirit.

Traveling around the world, she found her talent and lifetime career in photography. She learned she could elbow her way up to the front line — so essential in order to get "The Picture" in the Oval Office. She also learned to graciously defer her prized place to give her colleagues a crack at a good picture while falling into place within the hierarchy of the larger news organizations. After covering former President Clinton, Bowe stayed on at the White House to photograph former President George W. Bush, called "W" by reporters, and then former President Barack Obama.

Some of Christy's favorite quotes come from Carl Mydans and the late White House Press Secretary Tony Snow. Mydans said that by the time he began to use the camera seriously, he became "an obsessive people-watcher, observing mannerisms and body postures, the slants and curves of mouths, the falseness of smiles, the directness or evasions of the eyes." He added these were signals that he learned to interpret the human race. Snow once said, "The White House, with all its pressures, intrigues, triumphs, joys and disappointments, is the most special place you will ever want to work."

Bowe's photos say the same thing.

— **Helen Thomas**
Late Dean of the White House Press Corps

Chapter 1

She Who Would Not Be Ignored

Sarah McClendon
Bureau Chief
McClendon News Service

WITH A BOUNCE in my step, I headed off to my first White House News Photographers' Association (WHNPA) meeting. It was being held at the National Press Club (NPC) in Washington, D.C. I was thrilled to have become a member of the prestigious organization. I met up with a local Channel 8 cameraman on the way, and we wandered through the NPC looking for the meeting room. Neither of us had been there before, and somehow, we ended up in the Reliable Source bar. Someone at the bar apparently had "one too many" and told us that cameras were not allowed in that area and we needed to leave. Neither of us were shooting anything, we explained; we were just lost. When we finally arrived at our meeting, we told the others of our adventure.

A week later, both the cameraman and I received a letter from the president of the press club, Clayton Boyce, apologizing for the awkward situation along with an invitation to join the club and a calendar of upcoming events. Attempting to bolster my portfolio with a few notable names, I saw that Henry Kissinger was scheduled to speak there a week or so later. I arranged to have my tour of the club coincide with his speech, gambling that they would invite me to stay,

Chapter 1 | She Who Would Not Be Ignored

Sarah McClendon and Helen Thomas

> **Helen Thomas said, "She had guts. She asked the questions that should have been asked, and she asked questions for people who had no voice."**

and herded them into a single file line as we briefly morphed into a public-relations-type event. I eventually learned that that woman was the legendary reporter Sarah McClendon, "voice of the little folks" — the everyday, hardworking people. That night would eventually change my career.

Moments later, Henry Kissinger arrived, embraced Sarah and the two shared a personal moment, engulfed by a swarm of fans. Every photographer's nightmare then happened to me — my camera locked up during that big event. I was fortunate enough to capture a frame or two after moving on to my backup camera, casting the first into my bag in frustration. Luckily, I was able to fire off a couple more candid shots.

Days later, as I researched Sarah McClendon, I learned that she had accomplished some amazing breakthroughs in the news industry, including becoming one of the first women accepted into the National Press Club in the 1970s. A couple of those who had worked alongside Sarah had very nice things to say about their coworker.

Helen Thomas was quoted as saying that, "Sarah walked in where angels feared to tread. She had guts. She asked the questions that should have been asked, and she asked questions for people who had no voice. She made the veins stand out on President Eisenhower's forehead." Years later, President Bill Clinton remarked when asked about Sarah, "All of us who called on her in news conferences did so with a mixture of respect and fear, I suspect, because we would never quite know what she might say. I couldn't help but admire her spirit."

After learning all that, I decided to send her one of the pictures I had taken of her with Henry Kissinger, along with a note thanking her for "paving the road for us

and since I'd have my camera with me, it would be a good opportunity. That was exactly what happened.

The tour was quite brief, and I was then led into the famous Grand Ballroom to begin my temporary membership at the National Press Club. The cavernous room was filled with chairs in a theater-style fashion. I made my way to a front-row aisle seat, noticing there was only one other person in the room, and she was heading for the same spot. I got there first. The tiny woman with fiery-red hair ordered me to move to another seat because she wanted to sit there. I took that as a challenge and told her that I was taking pictures and had gotten there first. She initially seemed surprised and then mumbled under her breath, finally agreed and sat down next to me.

After the room began to fill up, people came by to greet that woman, some asking to have a picture taken with her. I wondered who she could be and decided to check it out. Before I could begin my investigation, I was thrust into the role of taking pictures of her with the various admirers. I organized everyone women who cover the news at the National Press Club" and telling her that I was joining the organization. A short time later, she called asking for permission to use my picture in a book that was being written about her life since leaving her hometown of Tyler, Texas. I agreed and offered to help her if she ever needed pictures for her company, McClendon News Service.

That began a whirlwind period of adventure in my life with Sarah. She would call and ask me to come with her to cover all kinds of events, from presidential press conferences to having lunch with Princess Diana.

As was frequently documented, U.S. presidents from Kennedy to G.W. Bush often seemed intimidated by her edginess and ability to get right to the point in a single question. She also made herself heard, her shrill voice persistently rising above the other reporters. Characteristically, Sarah loved to get manicures and would request the color she described as "violent red."

She always fought the struggle of the small news bureau — to be heard and respected and to thrive — a challenge that still exists today. She truly was the self-proclaimed "Citizen Journalist." She always managed to keep a friendly attitude, but if she didn't get a satisfactory answer, then all bets were off. One of the things I loved about Sarah was that she was always full of surprises.

One morning, Sarah and I were sitting in the White House Briefing Room when suddenly Sarah was tipped off that there was to be an impromptu question-and-answer session among select members of the media in the office of White House Communications Director George Stephanopoulos. As a newbie, I was unaware of what a special opportunity that was. Sarah said we had to quickly join the elite group of journalists that was quietly gathering.

Sarah McClendon and President Bill Clinton

Sarah McClendon and former President Gerald Ford

Sarah enters the Northwest Gate of the White House.

At that time, Sarah used a wheelchair and I had been assisting her as she taught me the ropes. We immediately began racing to Stephanopoulos' office with my cameras dangling from the handles of her wheelchair. We matched speed and passed our fellow reporters, and soon beat them as we made our way down the cavernous hallways to the chief of staff's office.

We rapidly secured our place at the conference table in a fashion similar to musical chairs and we each, surprisingly, snagged a seat. As those select reporters asked questions, my immediate instinct was to photograph the intimate exchange in that special place; however, that didn't seem appropriate, so I took out a small pad of paper from the bottom of my camera bag and pretended to take notes in an effort to blend in with the other reporters. Shortly after, Sarah asked me to see about getting my yearly credentials for Capitol Hill since I had to go back each month to renew the temporary 30-day pass. I had been going through that process for almost a year.

Upon learning what I had been doing for so long, she said, "Give me that phone. We're taking care of this right now." She called the superintendent of the Press Photographers Gallery of the Capitol at the time, Maurice Johnson, and demanded to know why her photographer had not yet received permanent credentials. What was the hold up? Her McClendon News Service was a legitimate media outlet. Maurice later told me that she could be heard down the hall from his office through the phone.

A couple of months later, after getting my Capitol Hill pass, I received my McClendon News White House hard pass and officially became a member of the White House Press Corps. Sarah knew how to get things done and had the best follow-through of anyone I have ever known. To have had her on your side and watching your back was the best insurance policy you could have asked for in this business.

One time, we were in a taxi on our way to a press conference at the White House and Sarah asked the driver what he would like to ask the president of the United States, if given the opportunity. The cabbie responded that he would ask for help with a family immigration problem. Forty-five minutes later, Sarah was asking the cab driver's question to the president of the United States on national television. She truly was the voice of the little people. For all the years I had worked with her, whenever we went to different events, everyone from Cabinet members to movie stars would come over and say hello to Sarah. Senator Alan Simpson put it like this at a roast held in Sarah McClendon's honor by the American News Women's Club: "Sarah knows how to tell somebody to go to hell and make them look forward to the trip."

As Sarah got older, she used a walker first and then the wheelchair. The White House did not have the best handicap access at that time, so when Sarah would arrive at the Northwest Gate press entrance, the Secret Service would open the double driveway gates for her, adding to the drama of her arrival.

She had earned a coveted seat in the White House Briefing Room — "McClendon News Service" engraved on a brass plate staking out her position. The press secretaries whom I encountered respected her but also seemed wary of her no-nonsense style of gathering information. Several years later, I talked with Sarah about starting my own little picture news service. She stood firmly behind me and supported me any way she could and celebrated my credentials as they transformed from McClendon News to yet another small news service: ImageCatcher News Service.

Sarah McClendon always believed in giving people a hand up. She certainly did that for me. All she ever asked was that I make the best of my talents, reach out a helping hand to others and "be sure to always keep an eye on the president." ✺

Chapter 2

My Shooting Style

I FELL IN LOVE with news photography while shooting a protest rally in Washington, D.C. It was there I met a UPI (United Press International Wire Service) photographer on the press truck and was invited to hop aboard and join the credentialed news photographers. I then discovered the fire in my belly — my passion for being where the action is and recording history as it happens.

Now I stand with pride, side by side with some of the most well-respected photographers in the country, as we prepare to shoot another event with the president of the United States. Over the years I have found that those of us who are small fish in the big pond of media outlets, often must compete harder to prove ourselves and earn respect. There are a few elitists who think themselves superior just because of the organization they work for, but for the most part, the Press Corps is made up of a great bunch of talented folks.

I have often wondered over the years how my small news organization, ImageCatcher News Service, got here. I have certainly put in my share of long hours and hard work covering the news alongside my fellow photographers. After all these years, I have learned the true value of what can be accomplished in a matter of seconds.

For many years, photo ops in the Oval Office were 10 to 20 seconds long, which demanded knowing the exposure and white balance settings prior to joining the fray. That allowed one to concentrate on positioning for the perfect shot and a moment to scan the room for other VIPs who may have been in attendance.

Oval Office encounters

Chapter 2 | My Shooting Style

A glimpse at the White House press photographers in the Oval Office.

Mark Zuckerberg faces both the Judiciary Committee and the press on Capitol Hill.

Although my company is minor, the history I witness is major and I am most grateful.

Each president had his own set of rules regarding media in the Oval Office. Presidents Clinton and George W. Bush were open to admitting the press into the inner sanctum of the Oval Office quite regularly, often with two waves/groups of photographers when meeting with special guests. President Barack Obama, however, put an end to having two waves/groups of media in the Oval Office so everyone had a chance at getting a photograph from various perspectives. That, unfortunately, carried over to the Trump administration. If one was lucky enough to get access during Trump's time in office, the president would allow the media to stay for longer periods, taking questions and making comments. He did, however, require us to have our cameras set on silent mode when taking pictures in the smaller venues like the Cabinet Room, Oval Office and the Roosevelt Room. Overall, with each administration, there had been a pattern of less and less access for most of the press who cover the president.

Although my company is minor, the history I witness is major and I am most grateful to all the photographers who have given me a break and shown me respect in our hypercompetitive, journalistic world.

14   EYES THAT SPEAK

Former Secretary of State Henry Kissinger meets with President Trump.

EYES THAT SPEAK

Chapter 2 | My Shooting Style

Marine One presidential arrivals.

> When it comes to editing, the power of cropping also helps to define the context of the picture when done either by our editors or us photographers.

Above: Proximity of Secret Service agents to the presidents; zoom lens captures the two presidents during the same scene.

I feel Maya Angelou's words say it best: "I come as one, but I stand for 10,000."

My camera has taught me to see, and when shooting pictures, I am concentrating on doing just that. I observe and attempt to predict what may be the one photographic moment that defines the story, whether photographing something as routine as the president's arrival on Marine One or Facebook CEO Mark Zuckerberg as he testified before the Senate on Capitol Hill.

Although many of the events I shot seem similar, each one was very different. The people defined each situation. As a news photographer, my days ranged from avoiding tear gas at a protest to receiving a compliment from President Donald Trump during a photo op.

Sometimes being a member of the media can limit access at certain events. I have learned over the years that, occasionally, it is better to put my press pass away and photograph with the general public.

I call that knowing "when to flash it and when to stash it." That could not have been more important than while photographing the insurrection on Jan. 6, 2021. Photographing the crowd at the Capitol, I came face-to-face with a group of the Proud Boys. They began yelling derogatory statements about the media while storming toward me. From that point on, I stashed my press pass under my jacket and worked as just someone else in the crowd taking pictures. The media came under

Presidents Obama and Clinton reunite for the AmeriCorps pledge ceremony.

EYES THAT SPEAK 17

Chapter 2 | My Shooting Style

Above: Washington, D.C., police drag an IMF protester from Freedom Plaza.
Top right: Palestinian supporters and protesters arrive on the Ellipse during the IMF march.
Opposite: Police officers dressed in riot gear face demonstrators during the World Bank IMF protesting activities.

attack that day as well. Some of us were threatened verbally, punched and cameras were smashed and even lit on fire.

In potentially dangerous situations, I prefer to travel light, take a chance and shoot with one camera body with a 28-300 focal length lens — using my iPhone 12 Pro cellphone camera as a backup. Thanks to the terrific new technology in cellphones, and carrying less gear, I can blend in easier and move more freely through the crowds. Now that I am more physically challenged, that is quite helpful.

When it comes to editing, the power of cropping also helps to define the context of the picture when done either by our editors or us photographers. Several years ago, I photographed Presidents Clinton and Obama at the White House for an AmeriCorps function. The two walked toward the Oval Office surrounded by their protective detail. In one image, Secret Service agents dominated, as opposed to the closer-cropped picture. Both had their merit; one was more inclusive, the other more private.

The mantra for press photographers is "hurry up and wait." During those moments,

Medics arrive to aid a protestor who was shot and later died during the insurrection at the Capitol.

there are opportunities to learn all kinds of cool trivia. For instance, one day while waiting to go into the Oval Office for a photo op, I was with a few seasoned White House Press Corps members discussing some of the amazing events we were fortunate enough to witness over the years. It was there I learned that the Secret Service assigns each president and his family code names that are used throughout their lives, e.g., Eagle, Trailblazer, Renegade, Mogul and Celtic. Much to my surprise, I found that this info was even on the internet!

Once the waiting ends and the shooting begins, I get "into the zone," shooting on reflex. I scope out details and the surrounding people in the room. I take a lot more pictures now that I can shoot hundreds of images digitally, unlike the film cameras we used for many years.

In the old days of film, we rationed our shots, always planning ahead for a "safe time" to change a roll of film. For every 36 frames of film, we always said, "There goes another roll." Always looming was the fear of needing to load film at a critical moment and missing the shot. This made it even more important to lug around multiple cameras as backup.

When I first began my career in photography, I would shoot a roll or two of black-and-white film, process it, make contact sheets in the darkroom, and bring them to my editors to select the image for publication. Today, as the president is speaking, photographers are simultaneously transmitting pictures to their editors around the world in a constant stream of breaking news.

Shooting about 5,000 to 10,000 images per month during busy times means that editing images has become more time-consuming. Every president I have covered has developed his own relationship with the media. For instance, President Obama seemed to give preference to the still photographers, while President Trump seemed to be partial to the TV cameras.

President Trump insisted that events held in the East Room of the White House would no longer allow the traditional TV lighting, which forced us to photograph using only the available low light cast by the chandeliers because the president believed that enhanced his appearance.

Since the beginning, there had been conflict between the press and the Trump administration. I was fortunate to be able to cover one of the rare, formal presidential press conferences that happened to be held in the East Room with less than one hour notice. CNN's White House correspondent „Jim Acosta, got into a heated exchange with the president after aggressively questioning him and ended up with his hard pass suspended. Following a court order, it was reinstated.

The president had been quoted many times as saying that the media was the "enemy of the people." Trump became known for holding rallies across the country that drew very large crowds. At those

President Trump answering questions at one of the daily COVID-19 pressers.

Chapter 2 | My Shooting Style

Members of the media have a temperature check before entering the White House grounds.

rallies, there often were negative comments about the media and the expression "fake news" and chants of "CNN sucks" were commonly heard. Several of the White House correspondents were forced to travel with a security detail to those events because the president got the crowds so worked up when he demonized the media.

For the press working inside the White House, things changed in the Trump White House. Spontaneity ruled. It was common for the pool to be summoned into the Oval Office, Cabinet or Roosevelt Room at a moment's notice. Being on site all day every day, when the president was home, was what it took to cover the Trump White House. As a small business, I did not have the luxury of either sitting at the White House all day or hiring someone to be there in case something went down. News was constantly being made, although we all did not have access to it regularly.

Most events became pooled press, but with special permission it was sometimes possible to cover a non-open press photo opportunity. If I was able to get in, there was more time inside the Oval Office or Cabinet Room to try and get the perfect shot because the president often made a statement and took questions, sometimes for up to 45 minutes if he was in the mood. He definitely had a few reporters that he liked to call on.

Presidential departures used to be mundane events. In the Trump White House, media swarmed to cover the departures; throwing elbows and climbing up six-foot ladders to see over the controlled chaos. President Trump would regularly come over to the press area and take questions on his way to Marine One. That came to replace formal press conferences and daily briefings. It became a more manageable way for him to have a give-and-take with the media. He was in control and could walk away at any time, unlike a traditional press conference where he was embedded with all of us for up to an hour or more.

We continued to have to respond via email to RSVP in order to cover a press event (requiring yet another press credential for that specific event).

Everyone put all those matters aside when the COVID-19 pandemic hit. Since the outbreak of the deadly virus, President Trump, VP Pence and his coronavirus task force began holding daily briefings in an attempt to keep the public informed of the ever-tightening restrictions. All media at the White House were ordered to have their temperatures taken and asked if anyone had had a fever or cough or traveled outside of the U.S. in the 30 days prior to entering the Northwest gate. They repeated the procedure at the doors to the Briefing Room, where we were given a color-coded sticker to wear that varied each day. Once inside, the Briefing Room seating was staggered as a protective measure against transmitting the virus. That became the crisis protocol for the unforeseeable future for anyone in close proximity of the president or vice president.

Daily media access to the president became routine, as he gave updates to the public with medical professionals by his side. That was covered exclusively by the White House pool.

It will remain to be seen, after this pandemic, if we will have more briefings and press conferences that are open to us all in the future or if more limited access is the new normal. ✪

Chapter 3
President William Jefferson Clinton

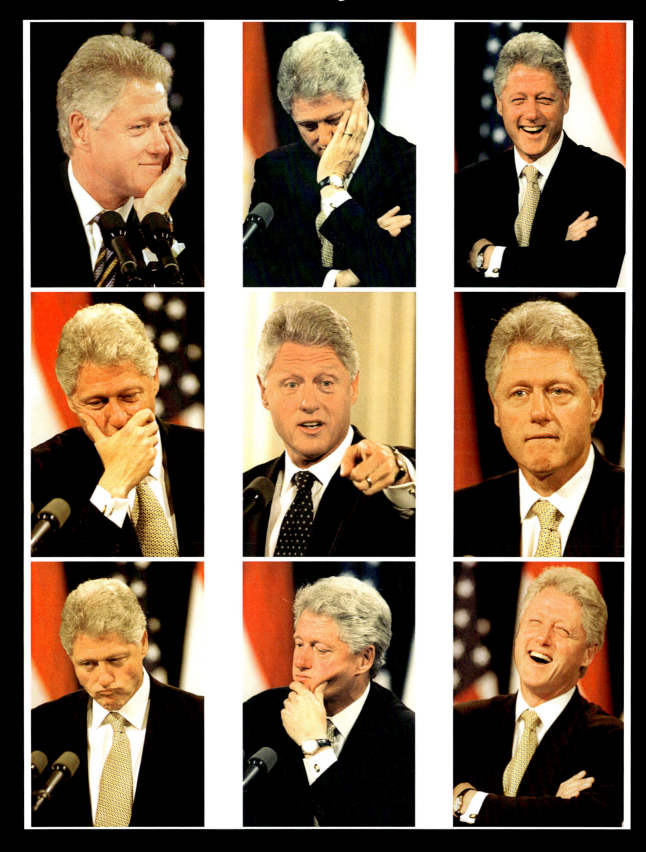

William Jefferson Clinton | Code Name: Eagle
January 1993-2001

THE FIRST TIME I WALKED through the gates of 1600 Pennsylvania Ave. solo was in October of 1994, and I was keenly aware of everything. As I approached the famous White House Briefing Room, a Press Corps reporter pointed out the bullet holes in the exterior wall of the building that were evidence of a crazed man on a shooting spree with a made-in-China SKS semi-automatic rifle. He had opened fire at the White House from outside the Northwest Gate. Earlier in May, President Clinton had banned imports of that same rifle. Reportedly, the president was the only member of the first family who had been home at the time. He was watching football on TV in the private residence when he heard the gunfire but was never in danger.

A couple of hours later, the media were escorted onto the South Lawn to hear President Clinton give remarks. Police tape and scaffolding still surrounded the old Andrew Jackson magnolia tree awaiting repair. Several weeks before, in the middle of the night, a 38-year-old truck driver had stolen a Cessna 150 and crashed onto the South Lawn of the White House, silently approaching with the engines turned off, startling the security detail who were on duty. Apparently, the pilot had been attempting to land on the South Lawn, but there were chairs and a stage set up for an event the following day, and the pilot crashed into the tree, which stood just a few feet from the house itself. The pilot died on impact.

Fortunately, the Clinton family had been staying at the Blair House while ventilation repairs were being made in the president's private residence at the White House. Yikes! Both events had occurred in a short period of time. I remember thinking, *What a unique introduction to the White House!*

I first began covering the White House during President Clinton's first inauguration, in 1993, even though I had not been inside the White House itself. Once President-elect Clinton arrived, I realized that my close-up spot at "the triangle" position was not so great for a photographer. It was closer than I had ever dreamed of but, sadly, due to the bulletproof glass surrounding him, all of the pictures were distorted. I was unable to use any of the images of the presidential swearing in that day. However, what a learning experience it was.

Proudly displaying my temporary Capitol Hill credentials, I moved on to test the waters with my newly acquired pass, wandering around the parade area and taking pictures of the participants. I managed to get other photos throughout the freezing morning and afternoon, but no more of President Clinton that day. Even though the bitter temperatures were very uncomfortable, the excitement of being on the front lines for the first time really helped distract me from the nasty weather conditions. Little did I know that, over the years, I would meet and shake hands with President Clinton many times.

Clinton had the reputation of being able to make anyone he was speaking to feel special and important. I found that to be true each time. I always assumed that it was due to having met him with Sarah McClendon — for whom I was originally working — that he was kind enough to give me a bit of special recognition.

In my opinion, President Clinton was a brilliant man. However, the scandalous Monica Lewinsky drama stood out in my memories of covering his presidency. On Jan. 26, 1998, the president claimed, "I did not have sexual relations with that woman, Miss Lewinsky," in a nationally televised White House news conference. Meanwhile in the press area, as various bits of information sifted into the Briefing Room, ABC reporter Sam Donaldson was one of the first to scoop Prosecutor Kenneth Starr's report, and he read aloud the spicier details of the document in his famous voice, as if he were reciting Shakespeare.

Since I was just beginning my post at the White House, I was vigilant in my coverage, even though my personal opinion was that that was between President Clinton, his wife and Monica Lewinsky. However, his lying under oath was another matter. Once the cover-up began unraveling, that changed everything for us members of the Press Corps. When that rumor became news in 1998, I needed to cover the historic process unfolding before the nation. As a small news agency, I had to be in several places at the same time. It was rewarding but exhausting.

As I gathered my wits and reached into my camera bag, I found I did not need that long lens after all. I was just two rows from the president.

Chapter 3 | President William Jefferson Clinton

Special Counsel Kenneth Starr briefs the media.

At one point, I got word that prosecutor Kenneth Starr was about to make a statement to the media outside of his office.

I waited there with a swelling crowd of photographers, TV crews and reporters. We were roped off to some degree, but there was not a lot of order to the mob. We patiently waited for an hour or two before Starr emerged and briskly walked right up to where I was standing near the gaggle of microphones. The crowd behind me surged forward, almost pushing me into him. I was so close that I had to keep backing up just to get him in focus with my short lens. That was my first successful stakeout.

Weeks later, on Dec. 19, 1998, at the Capitol early one cold morning, I put my stakeout skills to good use once again. Congress was voting on whether to impeach President Clinton for lying under oath. Many stakeout locations were set up at different places outside of the Capitol because no one was sure at which place any official statements would be made. I watched some of the more seasoned photographers and followed their lead, ending up at the southeast corner of the Capitol. After 13 and a half hours of debate in Congress, a decision was finally announced. With a flurry of activity, everyone flocked to where I was standing.

It felt like I had won the lottery. Members of Congress paraded down the stairs with a determined stride, stopping directly in front of me. Once again, I needed to step back to make sure I recorded that moment as history unfolded fewer than three feet away.

Six members of Congress announced that they were about to cast their votes on whether to impeach President Clinton and apologized for what the country was about to go through. Then they abruptly turned and proceeded back up the stairs to make their final decision. The reporter next to me was startled as he listened to his network earpiece. He then spoke into

24 EYES THAT SPEAK

the camera, "This is Patrick McGrath of Fox 5 News reporting live from the Capitol. President William Jefferson Clinton, the 42nd president of the United States, has just been impeached by the House of Representatives." A shiver ran down my spine.

I really needed to put it in high gear, so I rushed for the metro and then impatiently paced as I rode the train for 12 stops before arriving at the photo lab. I dropped off and waited for the film, placing an URGENT RUSH on my order to put me at the front of the line. Then it was back to my office to scan the film and transmit the selected images to my agency in New York. Those were the days of dial-up internet, and the process to get just six to eight images out took quite a long time.

While recovering from my long day, I sat in my home office after having finally let my loyal dog, Angel, outside. I was listening to CNN as I transmitted my images and heard correspondent Wolf Blitzer announce that President Clinton was about to respond to the media about the impeachment verdict.

To this day, I don't think I have ever moved so fast. I called the White House Lower Press Office to see if the "final escort" had taken place yet. Traditionally after a final escort, the media could not get in or out of the area where the president would be appearing. They said it was happening at that moment. I considered giving up, but something in me said I had to at least try to make it. The metro took what seemed like forever to get back downtown. Once there, I ran the two blocks from the train and sailed through the security checkpoint at the Northwest Gate at the White House. I saw that all the reporters, microphones in hand, were ready for action on "Pebble Beach," the area used in live broadcasts so that the north side of the White House was visible

Members of the House of Representatives speak to the reporters prior to voting to impeach President Clinton.

in the background. I ran up the driveway, and finally arriving in the Briefing Room, I flung the doors open only to find it empty. I had missed the final escort. Everyone was out in the Rose Garden! A plain-clothes Secret Service agent stood at attention with his back to me. I pleaded with him to just let me slip into the Rose Garden. He refused. I was pacing back and forth like a tiger in a cage when the doors suddenly flew open and

veteran-Associated Press photographer Scott Applewhite briskly walked in with the film he was to hand off to a courier. That event was huge.

"What's the matter? Are you locked out?" he asked me with just a touch of humor.

"Yes!" I exhaled in a pleading voice. Of course, he had no authority to get me past that agent, but I felt he was my only chance. Scott reminded me that I had no position in the crowded fray that had

Chapter 3 | President William Jefferson Clinton

President Clinton responds to the news of the House of Representatives voting to impeach him.

gathered outside the Oval Office and the press conference had already begun. I knew that all I needed was to get out into the Rose Garden a mere few feet away. I just needed a chance.

Scott turned to go back into the Rose Garden and was also stopped by the same Secret Service agent who refused me. Scott reminded him that he had been there all day and was with the AP. He needed to get back out there to do his job.

I followed behind him so closely there were only inches separating us. I made it! With adrenaline still pumping, I surveyed the large crowd and immediately worked my way around the perimeter and maneuvered up to the front, thanks to the gracious reporters who allowed me in their area. (All photo positions had been taken hours earlier.)

As I gathered my wits and reached into my camera bag, I found I did not need that long lens after all. I was just two rows from the president.

It was just about time for him to speak. Vice President Al Gore stood stoically behind President Clinton as first lady Hillary looked up at him with what appeared to be a tearstained face, strong in her resolve to get through that moment. That was how I saw it. The amount of guts and courage that it took to maintain a sense of dignity and pride spoke volumes about the first lady's own core strength. I imagine that had to be one of the most difficult moments in her life, as both her personal and professional lives collided in front of the world.

Racing home to repeat the same process, I was grateful to have my wonderful

The Clinton family leaves for vacation following the impeachment hearings.

President Clinton responds to the Senate verdict.

photo lab once again cooperate with me and agree to stay open late to process the film. That was one long day!

On Feb. 12, 1999, it was our job to wait for the Senate votes to come in. I can assure you that when it came time for the Senate to announce their decision, my ImageCatcher News Service was on top of it. I was not budging from the White House Briefing Room. After many hours of suspense, the Senate did not have enough votes to impeach, and we were all waiting to see if the president would make a statement. He could have spoken from the Oval Office with only one TV camera that would feed to the other networks, or he could have faced all of us in person. Suddenly someone noticed the special presidential podium being wheeled up the driveway. That signaled the president would make a statement in the Rose Garden. I was so proud to be one of the first in line to enter the Rose Garden that day, standing alongside legendary reporters Helen Thomas and Sam Donaldson.

President Clinton walked up to the

EYES THAT SPEAK 27

Chapter 3 | President William Jefferson Clinton

October 1998, Wye River Peace Agreement signing with Chairman Arafat of Palestine, King Hussein of Jordan, President Clinton and Prime Minister Netanyahu of Israel.

President Obama honors former President Clinton with the Presidential Medal of Freedom.

podium and stated, "Now that the Senate has fulfilled its constitutional responsibility, bringing this process to a conclusion, I want to say again to the American people how profoundly sorry I am for what I said and did to trigger these events and the great burden they have imposed on the Congress and on the American people."

As he turned to walk back into the Oval Office, Sam Donaldson yelled out, "Mr. President! Can you find it in your heart to forgive and forget?" There was an audible collective *aahh* from the Press Corps.

To our amazement, the president slowly turned, walked back to the podium and stated, "If someone is forgiven, they, too, must forgive." On our behalf, we were just delighted to get more of a reaction from the president.

President Clinton seemed to be bursting with relief and looked, to me, as if it were all he could do to not break into a dance. That was the one-sixtieth of a second that the media considered to have been the "nailed it" shot. Competing as we do, each

First lady Hillary Clinton is sworn in as a U.S. Senator of New York by Vice President Gore.

photographer fired away. Their camera and lenses met, and the views and the angles of that moment were shot around the world as each editor chose similar photographic images to publish.

Shortly after the vote, the first family headed for a private vacation in Martha's Vineyard. Many photographers gave witness to the first family's struggle. During the rest of his administration, I felt the president was never quite as friendly toward us, and our access was more limited. Still, President Clinton did know how to forgive us photographers from time to time.

For example, earlier in his administration, things got crazy in the Oval Office on two rare occasions that stand out in my mind. Secretary of State Madeleine Albright, gracefully sitting on the couch, was smacked in the back of the head with a large camera lens during a photo scrum with a visiting head of state. A week or so later, one of the wire photographers backed into the president's desk and knocked several of the first family's framed pictures on the floor. Those were the good old days of longer photo ops and more access, and plenty of forgiveness to go around.

The Clintons even honored the members of the press with summer picnics,

Chapter 3 | President William Jefferson Clinton

Secretary of State Hillary Clinton testifies at the Benghazi hearing.

once transforming the South Lawn into a carnival, complete with a Ferris wheel, merry-go-round and cotton candy. There were even various shooting galleries like the kind on the boardwalk at the beach.

We all knew that President Clinton's administration would be a turning point in American history. Clinton was the consummate diplomat, whether reaching out to us "annoying" press in his backyard or uniting conflicted world leaders at the Wye River Peace Treaty. His was a very significant time at the White House. Even President Obama recognized Bill Clinton's accomplishments by awarding him the Presidential Medal of Freedom in 2014.

The Clinton legacy, however, stems not only from the president but also from his remarkable spouse, Hillary. Beginning on Jan. 3, 2001, she was sworn in as a U.S. senator representing the people of New York.

After Bill Clinton's second term ended, the strong Clinton presence remained in the White House. In 2009, President Obama appointed Sen. Hillary Clinton as the new secretary of state. What a résumé she has! In 2013, she went on to become the most traveled secretary of state in history.

That same year, following a bout with pneumonia, she was challenged by members of the Senate Foreign Relations Committee during a blistering interrogation following the murders of U.S. citizens in the State Department who were stationed in Benghazi, Libya. The focus on that was later complicated by a scandal that erupted regarding Clinton's usage of an email server she had in New York for both her work as secretary of state and

Hillary Clinton is escorted to the hearing room among a flurry of media attention …

Representative Susan Brooks of Indiana questions Secretary Clinton on her emails.

Secretary Clinton testifies in front of Congress regarding her unsecured emails.

EYES THAT SPEAK 31

Chapter 3 | President William Jefferson Clinton

Above: Hillary Rodham Clinton and running mate, Tim Kaine, greet the cheering crowd after accepting her nomination for president of the United States during the 2016 Democratic Convention in Philadelphia, PA.
Left: Presidential candidate Hillary Clinton greets supporters during the National Democratic Convention.
Below: Daughter, Chelsea, and her father, former President Bill Clinton, listen as Hillary Clinton accepts her nomination and delivers her acceptance speech.

personal correspondence, which created a security risk. That time, Hillary Clinton faced off for eleven hours with the same members of Congress with whom she had worked side by side for years.

In April 2015, Hillary Clinton announced that she would make her second bid for the presidency, with strong support from her family.

The country was collectively shocked when, contrary to polls, she lost to Donald Trump in the long, close race. History continued to unfurl before the ever-watchful eyes of the Press Corps and the world.

Chapter 4

Growing Proud and Humble

Sarah McClendon and three of the twelve presidents she covered.

IF IT WERE A POKER GAME, would three "Mr. Presidents" and a "wild card" beat a straight or a full house? I had learned from Sarah McClendon how not to be intimidated by famous folks. Inside the National Building Museum, Presidents Clinton, Carter and Ford were preparing to sit down to a $1,000-per-plate dinner to raise money for the Truman Library. But first, they were to go upstairs to a VIP reception where those who had donated $10,000 each were afforded the opportunity of meeting those leaders and receiving a souvenir photo together. Sarah invited me to go to the reception with her. It was there that I learned only the current president has the title of "Mr. President." The predecessors are always referred to as "Mr." in the company of the current president.

I never dreamed I would have been in such a situation to learn that. Half seriously, I mentioned to Sarah what an opportunity it would be to get a picture of her with the three presidents. Sarah

**Truman Library Fundraiser
The National Building Museum
Washington, D.C.,
Oct. 25, 1995**

laughed and said it would never happen. I took that as a challenge and proceeded to hatch a plan to show Sarah just how much resourcefulness she had taught me.

The first former president to arrive was Jimmy Carter. He spotted Sarah in the crowd and went over to pay his respects. They chatted for a moment, and Sarah introduced me. I told Mr. Carter it was a pleasure to meet him. Then I added that I would like to photograph Sarah with him, President Ford and President Clinton.

I said, "You three would be representative of the many presidents Sarah has covered at the White House. The other two have already agreed. So, what do you

Chapter 4 | Growing Proud and Humble

Presidents Ford, Clinton and Carter pose for me at the Truman fundraiser dinner.

say, Mr. President, are you in?" He said yes and proceeded to greet other guests, eventually being swallowed up by the crowd. *Great*, I thought. *One down, two to go!*

Next to arrive was former President Gerald Ford. He, too, went right over to greet Sarah, who introduced me. That was the first of many times I would meet Ford. Both he and his wife had a special bond with Sarah based on mutual respect. I asked, and he readily agreed to my request. *Whoa! Two down, one to go!* But how would I get them all together?

Looking around, I saw that Carter had disappeared from the room, as did Ford. But to my delight, President Clinton entered. Security was noticeably elevated, and a red velvet rope separated him and the guests who had begun to form a receiving line.

President Clinton went over to greet Sarah and once again, she introduced me. Having twice practiced my sales pitch about the photo op, my confidence blossomed. I requested the picture and when he said, "Sure, we can do that!" I was thrilled.

One of his staff overheard this and informed me, "The two former presidents have gone downstairs already. I'm sorry." I joked that a Secret Service agent could talk into his sleeve and have the other presidents' protective detail bring them back because after all, "President Clinton said he would do this." Clinton heard me and with one glance, things began to happen.

In just a few minutes the two former presidents emerged and suddenly I stood face-to-face with all three, one asking where I would like them to stand. I was stunned that my plan had worked. Boldly, I gestured behind them to a few flags. "How about there?" I suggested. That same staffer said the three presidents would move Sarah to their side of the velvet ropes for the picture because she was wheelchair bound and that would be easier than getting her on the other side of that velvet rope. With shock and disbelief, I watched as my carefully orchestrated photo op benefitted the other photographers. The White House in-town travel-pool photographers fired away while I stood behind Sarah and the three presidents, watching my shot dissolve in front of me. I had gone from photographer to background, much to my dismay.

At that point, I jumped over the rope, while wearing a dress, and captured one frame before being elbowed out of the way by the Press Corps. The presidential trio then posed for pictures in front of the flags as I had suggested, and I briefly shot alongside the famously aggressive Press Corps.

Then, with wounded pride and a deflated ego, I stepped back over the rope to be redeemed by Sarah with praise and questions. Due to the noisy crowd, she of course had not heard the pitch to each of the presidents. When I told her, she had a good laugh about it. She said that she respected my guts, which was a huge compliment from the warrior of reporters.

I was then invited by a friend of Sarah's to join President Clinton's receiving line. When my turn came, the president, having seen the scuffle earlier, must have felt sorry for me and said, "Come over here," and then gave me a hug and posed for a special picture with me. That was a very kind thing to do, which I still appreciate to this day.

As I now reflect on that experience, I realize that what I did was not right. Lying and manipulating to get a picture is not how I want to conduct myself, but sometimes it is easier to ask for forgiveness than to ask for permission. Shortly after that, I also became a member of the infamous White House Press Corps. To this day, I, too, can "throw elbows" with the best of them. I have learned over the years, however, that it really does pay to be considerate of each other when you are on the front lines of history.

The favors you do for your fellow photographers and bystanders will be returned in kind. ✺

Chapter 5

Indebted to a Dynasty Icon

Rep. Connie Morella, Sarah McClendon and John F. Kennedy Jr.

ONCE AGAIN, I embarked on an adventure springing from an invitation from my bureau chief, Sarah McClendon. My assistant, Brian Yudd, and I were enlisted to bring Sarah to my first White House Correspondents' Association (WHCA) Dinner. I was not affiliated with the WHCA at that time.

When we arrived at the Washington Hilton, we found ourselves walking the red carpet alongside the various celebrities attending the event. Sarah was using a wheelchair, which allowed us special shortcuts and other perks, such as the elevator that let us bypass the person taking tickets.

The Correspondents' Dinner is a wonderful annual event in honor of the president of the United States. The press and the sitting president gently roast each other, awards for excellence in reporting scholarships are awarded to students and a good time is had by all. There are many receptions hosted by major news organizations and feature appetizers, cocktails and celebrities of all kinds, including former Cabinet members, rock and roll icons, movie stars, legendary athletes, publishers and comedians.

Brian, Sarah and I strolled along from one cocktail party to another, all the while

**The White House Correspondents' Dinner
Washington Hilton Hotel
Washington, D.C.,
Oct. 25, 1998**

being stopped by celebrity guests who wanted to meet Sarah or just say hello. At one point, even a Cabinet member stopped us to give Sarah a hug and quietly said, "Thank you for believing in me when no one else did. We girls are going to kick some ass here in Washington!" Personal greetings and well wishes continued from all levels of celebritydom as our little entourage made its way down the halls to my first WHCA annual awards dinner.

After a couple of hours, it was time to go through the magnetometer and have our gear searched. Before entering the huge ballroom where President Clinton, the first lady, the vice president, his wife, Tipper Gore, and many other VIPs were having dinner with members of the press, Brian and I had our cameras scanned through

EYES THAT SPEAK **35**

Celebrities abound on the red carpet at the White House Correspondents' Dinner in May 2009. Guests included filmmaker George Lucas, actor Samuel L. Jackson, musician Jon Bon Jovi and chef Gordon Ramsay.

security. We proceeded down a hallway where a WHCA staffer greeted the three of us, introduced herself and whisked Sarah away to her table. As we prepared to turn back, we realized we were inside without anyone asking to see a ticket. As we emerged into the giant dining hall, we suddenly became aware that we were rubbing shoulders with the world's elite.

The evening became surreal as network talk show hosts and other TV personalities asked us for directions to the restroom as we stood in the back just taking everything in, but somehow giving the impression that we belonged there.

We noticed a crowd of women giggling and pointing, and I thought they were pointing at Lord Earl Spencer, Princess Diana's brother, or rock star Jon Bon Jovi, but no, they were checking out John F. Kennedy Jr., who was there with the staff of his magazine, *George*. It was no secret that of the many presidents Sarah McClendon had covered, her hands-down favorite was John F. Kennedy, and I knew she had not seen his son, JFK Jr., since he was a boy.

Still in the process of building up a file of pictures of Sarah for books she was working on, I thought it would be fantastic if I could get Sarah and JFK Jr. together. The problem was that I did not know where she was sitting. To my disappointment, I finally learned that she was all the way across the enormous dining room. That meant she was several hundred people away from where we stood.

Nevertheless, I thought I would follow my own advice and ask the question. After all, the worst John F. Kennedy Jr. could do was say no. I waited for him to finish talking with a few more people before stepping up, introducing myself and shaking hands with him. I then asked if he would like to meet my bureau chief, a well-known reporter who had worked with his dad and his uncle Ted over the years. I had heard

Chapter 5 | Indebted to a Dynasty Icon

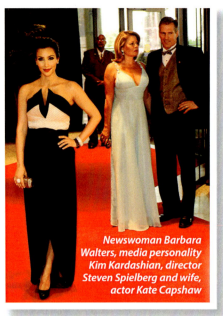

Newswoman Barbara Walters, media personality Kim Kardashian, director Steven Spielberg and wife, actor Kate Capshaw

Then I realized that during our brief time together, he had come to trust me in a small way, and I could not jeopardize that by picking up the camera that hung from my shoulder.

Senator Ted Kennedy tell Sarah, on more than one occasion, that she was like family, and I told JFK Jr. that. He thought for a few seconds, and said, "Okay."

I told him that I would bring Sarah to him. It would be a few minutes until I could get her back there because she was in a wheelchair. John insisted that we go to her instead. With that, we were off on our journey across the massive dining room with tables packed so tightly together that the waitstaff could barely get through in some areas.

During the first 50 yards, we must have been stopped at least five times as people, mostly women, asked to shake his hand and have their picture taken with little point-and-shoot cameras. I commented that it could take a really long time to get where we needed to go, and I asked if he wanted me to run interference for him. He enthusiastically said, "Sure! If you think you can do it." From that point on, as people stopped us, I told his fans that he was not able to talk right then. Smiling, I held firm with a "thanks for understanding."

As we made our way between the tables, he asked me to brief him on exactly who Sarah McClendon was. After I told him, I said, "You are going to get brownie points in heaven for going to all this trouble to make an elderly reporter's day." I proceeded to apologize on behalf of all the legitimate news photographers for the way his family had been stalked so badly by the tabloid photographers.

He then asked me, "What's in this for you?" I responded that Sarah was very special to me and that I knew her seeing him again would mean a lot to her. We finally got to the table, and Sarah was thrilled.

I gave them a private moment to speak, and I barely shot a couple of frames, before he was turning to leave, making the journey upstream back to his table. I felt Brian and I should have at least accompanied him back to his table after all of his efforts. On the way back, we ran into a friend of his from George magazine. We all stepped out into the hallway for a few minutes because dinner was being served and the aisles were so crowded.

We chatted casually for several minutes, and he kidded me, "You owe me big!" I suggested that he could "start me a tab."

When I asked him if he was stopped constantly when he went anywhere, he said, "Some days are worse than others."

As we joked around, I was thinking, *What great photographs I could make of these relaxed moments.* Then I realized that during our brief time together, he had come to trust me in a small way, and I could not jeopardize that by picking up the camera that hung from my shoulder. I felt that I needed to respect his privacy in that moment. I believed he was so comfortable around me and Brian because he knew we were not going to invade his personal space. And so, I held my fire and took no more pictures of John F. Kennedy Jr. that night. Or ever.

A little over a year later, he, his wife and his sister-in-law were tragically killed in a plane crash. Though I am a professional photographer, I realize that I will have to depend on my memories of that evening rather than on the special pictures that I might have captured of our small encounter. And I am just fine with that. I do owe him big. ◉

Chapter 6

Rendezvous With Royalty

THE MORNING BEGAN with a call from Sarah McClendon asking if I wanted to attend a press conference and have lunch with Princess Diana. The only catch? We needed to leave in 30 minutes. Little did we realize that this was to be Princess Diana's last visit to Washington, D.C.

The event was being held at the Red Cross Headquarters with 100 or so members of the media patiently waiting outside in the sweltering heat. We were kindly provided with box lunches and beverages while the princess dined inside with air conditioning and fine china. I did take comfort in the fact that we still had lunch at the same place and time, albeit under different circumstances.

Princess Diana was meeting with Elizabeth Dole in an effort to bring awareness to the dangers of old landmines that were still active in countries like Angola in central Africa. After several hours of waiting, the famous princess emerged from the building and strode across the courtyard to the podium. I was struck by the graceful way that she moved and the perfection of her appearance. She even sweated with dignity. That was the first time I had

Princess Diana
The Red Cross Headquarters
Washington, D.C.,
June 17, 1997

EYES THAT SPEAK 39

Chapter 6 | Rendezvous With Royalty

seen the famed Princess Diana in person, and I admired her composure.

Waiting for a cab after the event, a wheelchair-bound Sarah was shoved out of the way by the infamous "Royal Paparazzi." We were perched on a hill outside the Red Cross building, and she began rolling down the incline. I made a mad dash, catching her before any real damage occurred.

Those "reporters" stalked Princess Diana wherever she went, and I witnessed just how aggressive they were. They could make enough money to support their families for months from just one good picture of the princess. The more candid and private the moment, the more valuable the photograph. That type of photographer gives professional photojournalists a bad name.

Prince Charles and Camilla, the Duchess of Cornwall
The White House
Nov. 2, 2005

THE WHITE HOUSE schedule went out announcing that Prince Charles and his new bride, Camilla, the Duchess of Cornwall, were coming to the White House for a social visit. I was happy to have a chance to photograph more members of the royal family up close and in a respectable manner. Somehow though, the whole event was more low-key than I had imagined for a potential king.

As the royal limo pulled up at the South Portico of the White House, the two stepped out to greet the awaiting 43rd president and first lady, posing for about one minute for photos and then off they went for a private lunch. Later that evening they attended a formal black-tie dinner at the White House. The photo opportunity for both events was a little over two minutes.

Six years later, I was photographing Prince Charles in the Oval Office where he was meeting with President Obama. Only still photographers were allowed inside that time.

When photographing a visiting dignitary or head of state meeting with the president in the Oval Office, we are generally allowed inside either at the beginning (at the top) or the end (at the bottom) of the meeting. As a photographer and member of the White House Press Corps, I was always hoping to see those words in the Daily Guidance from the White House Press Office: "Still photographers only or photographers pool spray at the bottom." Although that was not often, it would mean my shooting time inside

would be up to a minute with plenty of space. I must say that over the years, the Oval Office opportunities have really taught me to focus on getting the job done in well under 60 seconds.

Queen Noor of Jordan
The National Press Club
Washington, D.C.
March 8, 2001

QUEEN NOOR is the only member of royalty that I have actually met and shook hands with. I was uncertain how to properly address her: was it, "Your Majesty" or "Your Highness"?

I went with Your Majesty. Being a firm believer in having a signature casual introduction, I decided on, "Hi, Your Majesty, my name is Christy Bowe, and I will be photographing you today for the National Press Club. If there are any special pictures you would like, please let me know."

The queen was on a mission similar to Princess Diana's visit. She was educating the public on the devastating global effects of landmines that were left behind in war-torn areas of the world. Queen Noor was, at that time, a patron and the chairwoman of the Landmine Survivors Network.

Sarah Ferguson,
The Duchess of York
The National Press Club
Dec. 7, 1994

SARAH FERGUSON, the Duchess of York, also had a cause. At the time I photographed her, she was in the process of raising money to help the children who were victims of the 1986 Chernobyl nuclear accident. After admitting to personal problems with her husband, she joked about getting in trouble from time to time. She then acknowledged that celebrities trying to improve their image sometimes assumed noteworthy challenges to deflect negative attention and hopefully hit a worthwhile target, giving focus to a worthy cause. Royal and ornery as she had been, I found it refreshing that, above all else, she considered herself a working-class mom.

Prince William,
The Duke of Cambridge
The Oval Office
Dec. 8, 2014

ONCE AGAIN, I found myself in the Oval Office with a royal. The prince had received a private holiday tour of the White House prior to my photo opportunity. Prince William, the Duke of Cambridge, had made a trip to the U.S. and decided to come to Washington, D.C. His wife, Kate, the Duchess of Cambridge, remained in New York. She had been expecting their second child and trying to limit her travel. My coverage of that event resulted in my picture being published in Time magazine. ☉

Chapter 7

Innocent Infiltrator
Swearing and the Swearing In of the 104th Congress

SINCE I HAD photographed Speaker of the House Newt Gingrich several times for McClendon News prior to getting any press credentials, I suppose he considered me a somewhat familiar face and we chatted amicably while strolling down the halls toward the House Chamber in the Capitol, my coat innocently slung over my camera bag.

At that time, Connie Chung had just aired her famous interview with Kathleen Gingrich, Newt's mother. Connie had wanted to know what Kathleen's son thought of first lady Hillary Clinton. The reporter had leaned in, whispering that her answer would be "just between you and me." The cameras had continued to roll as Kathleen replied, "The word rhymes with witch." That, of course, created quite a stir on the Hill, and press conferences were being held in different parts of the Capitol to better determine how the Speaker of the House really felt about President Clinton and his wife.

Personally, I think that the Speaker was probably glad to have a break from the media asking questions about the most recent drama. After all, I wasn't trying to get a response from him on the subject. We walked and continued small talk, passing several security checkpoints, until suddenly we rounded a sharp turn and entered the doors of the House Chamber room. The entire floor was bustling with excitement as the roll call of Congress was in progress. All I could think of was, *I know I should not be here, but what a great vantage point!*

As a temporary member of the House and Senate Press Photographer's Gallery, I was new to the workings of Capitol Hill and was not sure about all the rules just yet but could instinctively tell that I was in forbidden territory. No other photographers seemed to be anywhere near where I was; even Newt's wife was up in the balcony. I tried to find my way toward the back of the room and was soon ushered into a seat in the last row of the front section, which I eagerly accepted in an attempt to blend in.

As each name was projected on the screen and then called out with a validating "aye" response from each member present, I knew I was getting in deeper by the minute. The process was quite long and soon I began talking with the boy and his dad sitting next to me. The man introduced himself to me as freshman Congressman Mark Souder of Indiana with his son, Zachary. He asked if I would mind taking a picture of the two of them as he was sworn in as the new U.S. congressman of Indiana. His son was one of the only special guests I could see in my immediate area. Yikes! Sure, I would do it, but I realized that I could not use a flash. That was the era of film technology, which meant that I needed to switch to a roll of good old black-and-white XP2 film, so I could push it a couple of stops and use available light.

To my amazement, a short while later, all the people around me had stood and raised their right hands and were taking the oath of office. Getting into the spirit of things, I was tempted to stand up and do the same, just to fit in. Common sense prevailed, and I decided against it.

So, I guess I lost my only chance to become an "illicit" member of the House of Representatives. I

U.S. Capitol
Washington, D.C.,
Jan. 3, 1995

Chapter 7 | Innocent Infiltrator

shook hands, exchanged congratulations with the folks around me and tried to plan my escape. I assume they thought I was a family member of someone in my section. Either that or they just didn't care because they were wrapped up in their own moment.

A couple of days later, I got a call from Congressman Mark Souder, who politely requested a copy of the picture. I was delighted to have my first order from a member of Congress but realized that if he had that picture in his office and someone asked who took it, I could be in big trouble for being in a restricted area. I made an excuse that I would go through my files and look for it. By the next call from his staff, I am ashamed to say I lied and said the image did not turn out.

Many years later, as a law-abiding member of the House and Senate Press Photographers Gallery at the Capitol, I decided to tell Congressman Souder what had actually happened while I was photographing him at another event. I asked him if he still wanted a copy of the image. He did and was very understanding. Another year or so later while I was photographing former Speaker of the House Newt Gingrich, I told him this story and mentioned to him jokingly that maybe, had I raised my right hand, I could have been a congresswoman. He said that I may have made a pretty good one.

That lesson somehow reminds me of the latecomers at the movies who end up with a front-row seat, whether they like it or not. Although the larger-than-life view takes some getting used to, the experience reminds us just how small we really are. ✪

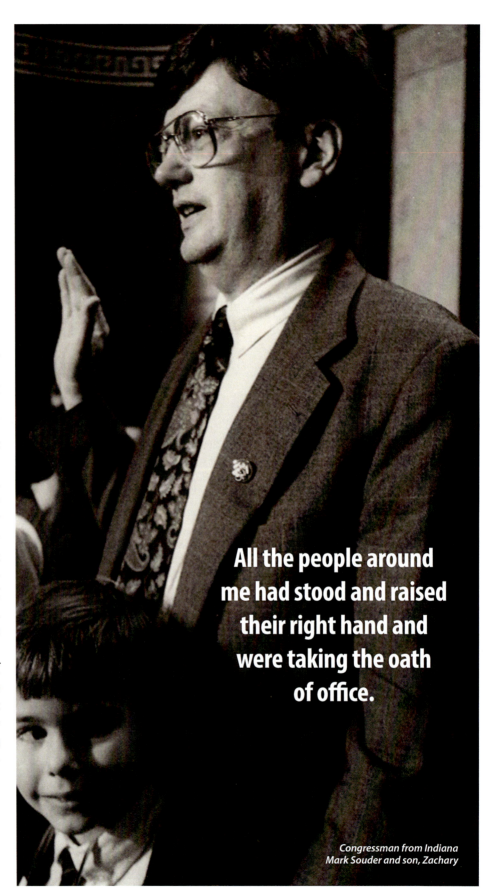

All the people around me had stood and raised their right hand and were taking the oath of office.

Congressman from Indiana Mark Souder and son, Zachary

44 EYES THAT SPEAK

Chapter 8

Peace on Earth
and Among the Press Corps

President George W. Bush, the Dalai Lama and Nancy Pelosi at the Congressional Gold Medal ceremony.

TENZIN GYATSO, the 14th Dalai Lama, was scheduled to receive the Congressional Gold Medal at the Capitol. That ceremony was the first time that the Dalai Lama was seen in public with a sitting U.S. president. Politics aside, that took a lot of courage from President George W. Bush.

For this historic event, many photographers from both national and international publications sought credentials and I had neglected to request a space when I should have but was grateful that I was allowed onto a lower riser position at the last minute. The event was held in the

**U.S. Capitol
Washington, D.C.,
Oct. 17, 2007**

House Rotunda of the U.S. Capitol with all the political who's who of Washington, D.C., in attendance.

As the Dalai Lama arrived on the stage, he greeted those who were about to speak, and thankfully, I was able to capture a few nice moments. After all the years in this profession, I have found that it always pays to be vigilant before and after the event that I am covering.

EYES THAT SPEAK 45

Chapter 8 | Peace on Earth

"You two, stop fighting!"

He connected with a total stranger and left behind a small oasis of peace and goodwill.

Oftentimes it is these moments that represent history the best. For instance, the Dalai Lama was able to ease the tension between the Republican president of the United States and the Democratic Speaker of the House of Representatives into shaking hands with each other prior to the ceremony.

After several speakers made their remarks, it was time for the presentation of the Congressional Gold Medal. As President Bush turned to present the award, hundreds of people in the audience stood up and raised their cellphones over their heads to take a picture, in effect blocking us professional photographers who were near ground level. (This is increasingly problematic during public events everywhere, now.)

Disappointed, but not defeated, I was herded outside with many other photographers to position ourselves for the photo op of the Dalai Lama coming down the stairs of the Capitol to greet the crowd of monks and followers from around the world.

A secure area was formed for credentialed media, where we were instructed by Capitol Police: "Hold here, no matter what" until His Holiness passed by and ascended onto the six-foot-high stage area. After about 30 minutes, he came down the west steps of the Capitol. One of his attendants held a huge umbrella that covered the Dalai Lama almost completely to protect him from the sun and heat. We

The Dalai Lama with Whoopi Goldberg.

watched him embedded within his entourage, passing us by without any hope for a decent picture, once again.

Spinning around quickly, I noticed some of my fellow photographers in position directly in front of the stage where he was headed, camera shutters firing like machine guns. Several of us asked the Capitol Police why we were being held back while our competitors were free to shoot away.

The officer told us to "stand down."

After several minutes, with the adrenaline rushing from the frustration of missing yet another opportunity, I took matters into my own hands and headed for the stage. That was, of course, not allowed and could have invoked serious consequences, but I sprang into action anyway.

Dashing to the stage where the Dalai Lama was already engaged with the media, I came upon a crowd about 10 people deep. Fortunately, a space appeared right up front, and I immediately jumped

into that spot, not realizing that a bunch of photographers were on my rear flank. Those behind me abruptly rammed into me which shoved me into the photographer in front of me. She spun around and angrily snapped, "What the hell are you doing?" I responded that I couldn't help it, I had been pushed from behind.

His Holiness, the Dalai Lama, ever the Ambassador of Peace, hobbled to the edge of the stage, wagged his finger at the two of us and said, "You two, stop

EYES THAT SPEAK 47

Chapter 8 | Peace on Earth

fighting!" He said that in a genial and joking way, and we all went back to our business.

Little did I realize that His Holiness was about to give me a special opportunity. After taking a few images of the entertainers and their opening remarks, I prepared to leave and took one last look around. A crowd was forming by the side of the staging area, and as I have learned over the years, the best way to a good vantage point in that situation is to weave your way around the perimeter of the crowd and begin to work inside to the front lines. Before I knew it, I stood just a few yards from His Holiness. He sat in a chair watching the performers on the stage. Our eyes locked as he winked at me. I let my camera down onto my shoulder and put my hands together in the international prayer gesture and said, "Namaste," ("I greet the God within you") which I had learned while in Kathmandu. I cocked my head to the side and smiled, conveying, *Can't we just put that earlier incident behind us?* He turned and posed for me as his smile erupted into laughter.

At that moment, I felt a strong connection with my subject and believed that a lesson was learned: persistence paid off. As the old saying goes, "It is not how many times you are knocked down, but how many times you get back up." I realize, looking back, that even an icon can be understanding of somebody else's tough day on the job.

The good karma between the Dalai Lama and I continued years later, when I photographed him again on the west side of the Capitol as he made remarks and was interviewed by Whoopi Goldberg. That time, I was well prepared for any obstacles. I had secured my special credentials for that event in advance, and when it was time, I moved into a great spot in the press pen close to the stage. Since that was an event that did not have a lot of other VIPs, it was much more laid-back, security wise. I even invited a young, novice photographer into the press pit to take a few shots because there was plenty of room, and I wanted to take my good fortune and pay it forward.

As I stood at the Capitol on that blistering hot July morning, I thought back to my previous encounter with His Holiness and came to understand that man really lived his faith. Encountering unexpected strife in the midst of a public event, he had gently — and with humor — defused it. He connected with a total stranger and left behind a small oasis of peace and goodwill.

Namaste. ✺

Chapter 9

President George W. Bush

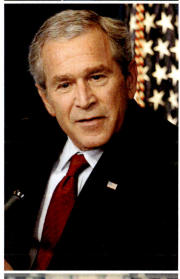

George W. Bush | Code Name: Trailblazer
January 2001-2009

I BEGAN COVERING George W. Bush during the Gore vs. Bush election controversy outside of the U.S. Supreme Court. Democrats, Republicans and other American citizens stopped by the nation's highest court to express their opinions on the potential miscount of votes for the 2000 U.S. presidential election.

There were plenty of creative signage and chanting, and a blanket of police presence. Flashing my press pass, I crossed over the police lines and onto the steps of the Supreme Court, observing the controlled chaos.

The security detail stepped aside as they checked for credentials and allowed me through the restricted area — one of the cool parts of this job. It made me feel special for a brief time until I mingled with my people, where we had formed our own hierarchy. I stood alongside some national award-winning photographers, who were more accomplished than I, yet we were shoulder to shoulder on a regular basis.

I photographed both of the George W. Bush swearing-in ceremonies. Once again, the weather was the cold, colder and coldest temperatures of the year with some freezing rain added into the mix. I think everyone has noticed that on non-inaugural years, the weather usually was not nearly as bad as it was during swearing-in ceremonies in Washington, D.C., on Jan. 20.

President G.W. Bush's first inauguration came with an additional layer of stress because I had agreed to photograph the presidential motorcade for my client, Harley-Davidson. The motorcycles were in a V formation surrounding both the presidential and vice-presidential limos

Police in riot gear at George W. Bush's first inauguration.

during the inaugural parade. They wanted the image to include a Washington, D.C., landmark — the U.S. Capitol. I chose the view down Pennsylvania Avenue at Freedom Plaza. My assistant and I had gone down about a week before, and I had showed him the exact spot that I needed him to save for me. Although I had warned him, I do not think he realized that it would mean literally standing in icy conditions from dawn until dusk to hold my precious place. The preplanning aspect of doing a walk-through to determine the correct angle and strategize the best way to get from one point to another in challenging conditions is critical.

Earlier at the Capitol on that Inauguration Day, all pre-credentialed photographers were instructed to be on the grounds before dawn. We were also required to have a $1 million liability policy for the day, lest we fall down and hurt ourselves, and sue the Washington, D.C., government. So, on the day of Jan. 20, I was worth a million dollars ... me! A million-dollar photographer!

Sweet.

Covering the first Bush inauguration with a closeup position was very exciting. As the president took the oath of office, I held onto my camera with cold, numb hands, hoping I could press the shutter fast enough even though I could not feel my fingers. I was thankful for the opportunity to be present with a bird's-eye view as the son of a former U.S. president was sworn into office.

I was a bit stressed about how I would get to my next position for the inaugural parade. Immediately following the swearing-in ceremony, I jumped into action, implementing the plan I had formed a week earlier. I began the chess-like strategy needed to work my way down to Freedom

continued on page 55

The inauguration of President George W. Bush, January 2005

The presidential motorcade starts off the inaugural parade.

Inaugural parade route protesters and (right) presidential protective detail escort, 2001.

Plaza, where thousands had been standing for up to 12 hours, shoulder to shoulder.

A normal 20-minute walk became a four-hour obstacle course due to the crowds and street closings. I approached my position covered in muck from trekking through the over-trodden, soggy patches of grass that had been reduced to mud. I was tired, soaking wet, hungry, thirsty and in desperate need of a restroom without a long line. After several hours searching for a point in the road where anyone was allowed to cross the street, press included, I ended up having to go past Freedom Plaza for eight blocks then had to double back those same eight blocks on the opposite side of the street. The security was ratcheted up because the protesters who disclaimed the final vote count in the Gore vs. Bush presidential race were actively demonstrating.

After a few hours of struggling to get through the thousands of spectators while carrying all of my camera gear and a small ladder, I had to remind myself to keep pushing, searching for a second wind. Then I panicked as I heard the marching band, which signaled that the presidential motorcade was approaching. To hurry up, I used my monopod as a cattle prod, so to speak, to gently forge a path through the crowd. Looking ahead, I was about 50 yards from my goal.

Hours after having left the ceremony, now exhausted, I pulled myself up onto the press riser behind a newscaster. She wore a flashy red outfit and was perfectly made up, hair totally composed, with an assistant holding an umbrella as she waited to go "live" on the network. She stepped aside giving me more than ample room so that I wouldn't get her outfit dirty, I assumed.

Living Hall of Fame baseball players visit the White House for lunch.

My stringy hair, still damp from 12 hours of sleet and rain, mud-caked pants and shoes and makeup, having streaked my face hours earlier, provided stark contrast with other members of the media around me on that platform.

Gathering up my dignity and wiping the hair out of my face, I stepped into my waiting position and immediately began shooting as the presidential motorcade came into view.

It was only because President Bush was running late that I was able to make my deadline to my clients with only minutes to spare. Traditionally the inaugural parade could not start until the previous president was "wheels up" in his plane. Former President Clinton's many goodbyes were the holdup. Some speculated the delay was retribution for the vote count, but who knows.

By the next Bush inauguration, I had a much better plan and elicited help from both the District of Columbia Police Department and the Federal Park Police along with special assistance from Harley-Davidson. I was fortunate to have a predesignated officer who arranged for me to ride in a squad car to my position at Freedom Plaza, empowering me with a sense of importance, whether I deserved it or not. Although I had no official press pass for a position along the parade route that day (I had given my only parade credential to my assistant, so he could hold my spot), I hoped that I would be able to cross police lines anyway because I was with an officer.

The squad car dropped me off on the correct side of the street at the barricades, and the police officer checking credentials chatted with his fellow officer. Since I got out of the police cruiser, he did not bother to see if I had a pass. This caused a bit of a buzz among the other out-of-town photographers in my area, as I gained celebrity status with my arrival up on the press platform. I attempted to lay low for the next few hours, hoping no one would ask any questions. I basked in my good fortune as I reminisced about the previous inaugural situation.

The U.S. Secret Service gave President Bush the code name "Trailblazer," probably because he loved to do the physical work of clearing the brush on his ranch in Crawford, Texas, whenever he had a little downtime.

Because I had not previously witnessed a transition at the White House, the change was unsettling. I was apprehensive about what to expect from the new White House residents.

My fears about covering this new president were put to rest in the first week. He invited all of the living Baseball Hall of Famers to the White House for lunch. As a former owner of the Texas Rangers, he expressed that he had always been a big baseball fan. So, those men had been his heroes when he was growing up, and some still were. As the president stood in the East Room with a riser packed with baseball champions, he admitted that he had come to realize that because he was president of the United States, he could invite those legends of the sport to come to the White House and they probably would accept the invitation. He was right. Not only did they come, but they came bearing gifts. One was a baseball bat that they had all signed. Imagine what that is worth today!

I was also charmed by the close relationship the new president had with his family. Both he and his father had baseball caps numbered 41 and 43, symbolizing their positions as presidents of the United States.

President Bush, at sunrise, awaits the Olympic torch.

The president and first lady prepare to welcome Queen Elizabeth II.

Several years later, while photographing the elder Bush, also known as Papa Bush, I gave him my favorite picture of his son wearing a cowboy hat at sunrise on the South Lawn of the White House, which I had taken in 2001. I was surprised when the former president sent me a nice, handwritten thank-you note signed "George Bush #41." I keep that memento proudly displayed in my office today. It impressed me that someone of his stature would make such a thoughtful gesture.

It was during this Bush administration that I begrudgingly made the transition to the world of digital photography. My first hard lesson in the digital world came the morning of Sept. 11, 2001, when terrorists suddenly attacked our country. Now we were at war. I went to grab my gear and my batteries were dead. While I waited the 30 minutes or so for a charge to take hold before I rushed to downtown Washington, D.C., I learned that first the twin towers were hit and then the Pentagon, followed by Shanksville, Pennsylvania. The Pentagon was sealed off within minutes to anyone not having a Pentagon pass, like me. In the panic of the moment, broadcasters incorrectly announced that the Old Executive Office Building had been hit and that the White House was the next target. Following the orders from my editor, I rushed downtown — as did many members of the media, despite the possible dangers — to cover that breaking news. Fortunately, the trains were still running. As I got off at the metro station nearest the White House, I saw Roland Mesnier, the White House pastry chef, standing in the middle of Farragut Park with other members of the kitchen staff still in their white uniforms. Everyone was rushing to leave downtown while first responders and news people were doing just the opposite. Some of the same officers I routinely saw were now holding machine guns. They pushed us back from the White House one block at a time. As a crowd, we stood united, searching frantically to make cellphone contact with our loved ones and our editors.

The cars surrounding us were being checked for bombs, others towed away

The Pentagon offices on Sept. 12, 2001.

Moment of silence at the White House, Sept. 11, 2002.

EYES THAT SPEAK

Presidents 41 and 43 leaving Marine One.

from their parking spaces, because all routine behaviors were now suspect. Having never experienced being at war before, I kept thinking about my dad's WWII stories and thought, *This is it*. The controlled panic in the streets did not provide me with any spectacular images that day and so I went home.

The next morning, however, I made my way to the Pentagon, where a media area had been set up to relay the nightmare that had happened the day before. The devastation was sobering as I focused my lens on the exposed desk, chair and file cabinet which appeared relatively untouched, where a worker had been sitting as the exterior walls had been blown off the building. We all attempted to find meaning in the pictures we were taking as we struggled to stay professional by concentrating on shutter speeds and composition.

Two months later, I photographed one of my favorite images of President Bush as he stood outside the South Portico at sunrise, awaiting the arrival of the Olympic torch. To me, this Texas sentinel portrayed the image of a cowboy looking out on "his herd." That proved to be a very powerful and emotional moment as the torch was handed off that morning.

In the years following 9/11, there have been many memorial services and prayerful moments of silence. During that period, the most significant to me was on Sept. 11, 2002. The Bushes and Cheneys emerged from the White House surrounded by all the White House staff, including the administrative employees, housekeepers, chefs and groundskeepers. That moment of silence was deafening with meaning.

There were many other celebrated events during the Bush years, and one of the most momentous was a visit from Her Majesty, the Queen of England. The affair was very carefully planned, and protocol reigned. Thanks to then-Secretary of State, Condoleezza Rice, it was a white-tie affair.

While covering the White House

during the #43 Bush administration, I had the most memorable personal exchanges with any U.S. president to date. During the Bush administration, when photographing in the Oval Office, we normally had anywhere from 10 to 20 seconds (for us non-pool photographers) to take a picture of the president who, generally, is sitting with another visiting head of state in front of the fireplace, our president on the right and the visiting guest on the left. We traditionally would hear a voice from one of our handlers stating, "Thank you very much, ladies and gentlemen." That is our cue to depart. It is an unwritten law among us that photographers do not ask questions and reporters do not take pictures. Fair enough. The only exception to this rule is if the president should happen to speak to you first. I was fortunate enough for that to have happened to me several times.

In fact, President George W. Bush and I had some of my favorite one-liner exchanges in the Oval. For example, while I was leaving a photo op in the Oval Office, and was the only woman photographer present for the event that day, the announcement was made:

"Thank you, gentlemen."

The president commented, "There are not only men here, you know."

I replied, "Thanks for noticing, Mr. President."

He responded, "I always notice," and winked.

It was fun joking around with the president of the United States.

President Bush did not make me feel like there was a big difference between the most powerful man in the world and the smallest photo news bureau at the White House. He gave the small folks a break with some special attention. I respected that. A lot.

Shortly after his re-election in another

The first family celebrates the second presidential victory.

photo op with then-Prime Minister Tony Blair in the Oval Office, President Bush asked, "Hey, did you guys vote for me?" as he looked in my direction.

I was taken aback, but answered, "Why, yes I did, Mr. President."

He replied incredulously, "Really? You did?!" A great natural, unscripted moment ...

Christmas parties for the press have always been a treat at the White House. Members of the press were allowed to mingle freely on the State Floor as we were offered a wonderful array of food and drink. If invited, each of us could bring a guest, and part of the fun of the evening was that we met the president and had our picture taken by the White House photographer. When it came time for my picture, the line of guests snaked down the hallway. I eventually reached a Marine in dress uniform who asked how to correctly pronounce my name and that of my guest for the introduction to the president. A few feet farther and I was standing face-to-face with the president and first lady.

Another memorable exchange was the 2007 Christmas party. I brought a friend who was a Catholic priest as my guest. As the president greeted me warmly, he looked over my shoulder at

continued on page 64

The Bush family and the nation pay tribute to former President George H.W. Bush.

EYES THAT SPEAK 63

President Bush welcomes the prime minister of Australia.

"To those of you who received honors, awards and distinctions, I say well done. And to the C students, I say you, too, can be president of the United States."

my friend who was wearing his Roman collar. President Bush suddenly became quite serious and as he shook hands with the priest, he asked him to please pray for him and everyone in the White House.

As the final Bush Christmas party rolled around and I greeted President Bush, I said to both him and the first lady that I would miss seeing them around the White House all the time. Out of nowhere, President Bush reached out and gave me a big bear hug, and as he rocked me back and forth in a paternal kind of way, he kissed me on the cheek and the forehead. Were there any pictures of this? No. Where is a good photographer when you need one?

Once, while speaking to students, he said, "To those of you who received honors, awards and distinctions, I say well done. And to the C students, I say you, too, can be president of the United States." I always appreciated his sense of humor.

On Dec. 4, 2018, I witnessed former President George W. Bush saying goodbye to his dad, former President George H.W. Bush. A lone drum was heard through the loud silence as the casket was brought down the stairs of the U.S. Capitol and the traditional president's song, "Hail to the Chief," was played one final time by the Marine Corps Band as the 41st president was placed in the presidential hearse.

I feel privileged to have had a special glimpse of the human side of our 43rd president whose father also sat behind the desk in the Oval Office. These presidents are still people with feelings and what they do in every aspect of their lives is up for scrutiny. For those chosen few, however, it will be up to the history books to decide how they are remembered.

Chapter 10

Diamonds, White Ties and Tiaras

THE VISIT OF Her Majesty Queen Elizabeth II and His Royal Highness Prince Philip, Duke of Edinburgh, to the White House seemed to excite everyone from the president and first lady to the waitstaff — even the press. This visit was the first of the two grandest events I have had the honor of covering in my White House career.

Although the routine was much the same as any other state arrival, this was the Queen of England. Her face was on money!

We were advised that our preset would be at 7:30 a.m. Although we got on brilliantly with most of the members of the British Press Corps, a few of them were prepared to do anything for the price of a picture. They were the famous tabloid photographers who followed the royals wherever they went.

The formal arrival ceremony went exactly as planned with all the pomp and circumstance expected. The sense of awe at being in the presence of royalty with all the glittering diamonds and ramped-up security added to the excitement of this royal visit. Unfortunately, aside from all the anxiety of getting everything just perfect for the queen, her visit was actually sedate. Everything was so overplanned and scripted that it seemed there was little room for a natural moment.

continued on page 68

Queen Elizabeth II
The White House
May 7, 2007

The military honor guard prepares for the arrival of Queen Elizabeth II.

Chapter 10 | Diamonds, White Ties and Tiaras

As we waited for our escort for the State Dinner arrival preset, a few of us got to talking about what the queen's life must have been like. I, for one, was fascinated that she carried a purse everywhere. So, what was in that purse? More diamonds? A handgun? Breath mints? Earlier in the day, at the arrival ceremony, prior to her speech, she had opened her purse; we had eagerly zoomed in to catch a peek inside but had only spotted her reading glasses. At least we knew one item that was stashed in there.

I spoke with another photographer about this mystery. She was a working White House photographer who attended a state arrival for President Bush (41) at Buckingham Palace, and lo and behold, the queen appeared and greeted the president, inside the palace with her purse!

Legend has it that she used it to signal her handlers by moving it a certain way to communicate her wishes, such as "leave us alone" or "get this person away from me."

As members of the press, we sometimes delve into what we think the subjects' lives are like as we stand around in the various holding areas. I speculated that this royal woman, so young when crowned, was raised in a cocoon while being educated in "courtly" behaviors, with no opportunity for a "normal" childhood.

Wow, was I ever wrong! I was quite surprised to learn that while growing up during WWII, Her Majesty went out among the people and worked alongside other female volunteers as a mechanic for several months. Who would have guessed that this impeccable icon, in her diamond tiara, would ever have had grease under her fingernails?

Also, on the personal side, I learned her interests included spending time with her Welsh corgi dogs as well as watching a good wrestling match or horse race!

Sometimes lessons happen while we are waiting for life to unfold before us.

It had been five hours since the first arrival ceremony at the White House, and members of the media waited across from Pebble Beach as more photographers continued to join the swelling crowd. Normally we all queued up at the bottom of a long flight of stairs that funneled us up as we all dashed to the North Portico of the White House, speed determining our chance at a good position. On that day, however, we all stood anxiously on the open sidewalk of the North Lawn like horses waiting for the start of the race.

I was concerned about the bedlam that would ensue once we were given the go-ahead to move forward to claim our spots. Once given the go-ahead, everyone set off in a full sprint similar to a childhood 100-yard dash, only there were cameras, stepladders and bodies colliding in the frenzy as we competed for a good position to view the royal couple's arrival for the State Dinner. I proudly secured a spot in a decent location. At last Queen Elizabeth and Prince Phillip stepped out of their SUV just a few yards away and were greeted by the president and first lady as the thunder of dozens of cameras fired away.

The saying goes that pictures don't lie. I realized that preconceived notions really did put a filter on the lens of my camera that day, and that distortion kept me from seeing the real truth about my royal subject.

President Bush and first lady Laura welcome Queen Elizabeth II and Prince Philip.

Queen Elizabeth II makes a sparkling arrival at the White House.

Chapter 11

From Prisoner to President

NELSON MANDELA WAS the first president of any country that I had ever met. He was also the first Nobel Peace Prize recipient I had photographed. Prior to his speech, I had an opportunity to meet him at a reception. With the signature trademark of other great leaders, he looked me in the eye — as if I were the only person in the crowded room — focusing his total attention on me, as we spoke briefly and shook hands. He had a good, firm handshake yet projected a gentle quality that was surprising to me because he had just recently spent 27 years in prison. His bright sense of humor seemed to twinkle in his eyes. He had once quipped during the height of President Clinton's personal impeachment scandal, "In my

President Nelson Mandela
of South Africa
The National Press Club
Oct. 7, 1994

country we go to prison first and then become president."

Later, from my vantage point a few feet from the podium, I listened as he spoke about his determination to forgive his captors and move on with his life. Although his delivery that day was halting, his message was steady and well crafted.

Then, with presidential demeanor, he outlined concrete plans to remove the lawlessness in his country, spoke of strengthening an emerging infrastructure so that even remote South African villagers could

Nelson Mandela at the National Press Club.

Nelson Mandela in the Oval Office in May 2005.

benefit from democracy and urgently sought investments from the world's business leaders. I realized he repeatedly deflected questions so that his personal fame did not overshadow his message. One of my favorite quotes of his was: "I learned that courage was not the absence of fear, but the triumph over it. The brave man is not he who does not feel afraid, but he who conquers that fear."

His tone and body language clearly exhibited the strength of his convictions and of his plans for a democratic South Africa. He insisted that he have an elected successor so that riots would not rock the streets upon his death.

Eleven years later, I was allowed to photograph him again in the Oval Office with President George W. Bush. He announced that this was to be his final visit to the U.S. Although he had changed, both in title and appearance, his message was strong, even as his then-frail body was failing.

To me it seemed that as he made his way around the world saying his goodbyes to various leaders, he projected a calm certainty that came from fulfilling his destiny. ✺

As he made his way around the world saying his goodbyes to various leaders, he projected a calm certainty that came from one who had fulfilled his destiny.

Chapter 12

An Encounter With James Bond
Secret Agent 007

I WAS THRILLED to get the assignment to cover Sir Sean Connery, aka James Bond, Secret Agent 007, for the National Press Club at an early morning event known as the Morning Newsmaker. The NPC program moderator and I met the actor and his wife, Micheline Roquebrune, as they were exiting their limo. Sir Sean towered over his petite wife. I was surprised to learn that she was a mature woman and a talented French Moroccan artist with a great sense of humor, and not the buxom, flutter-brained "trophy girl" that the character James Bond might have chosen. Connery was about to speak to journalists on tourism in Scotland and the problems the country had endured with mad cow disease.

As we made our way up to the 13th floor of the Press Club, our little entourage was stopped constantly as the adoring fans gushed with excitement. The amazing thing to me was that those were mostly men with one thing in common: they all had huge "man crushes" on the real James Bond, as he had been christened over the years. One man even asked him, "Would you like a martini, shaken but not stirred?" It was 8 a.m. and Connery declined the offer, but to have had that exchange was clearly a dream come true for that gentleman.

Sir Sean Connery
The National Press Club
Washington, D.C.,
April 6, 2001

EYES THAT SPEAK 73

Chapter 12 | An Encounter With James Bond

April 6, 2001
Sir Sean Connery and his wife, Micheline Roquebrune.

They all had huge "man crushes" on the real James Bond, as he had been christened over the years.

After a few of those encounters, I remarked that it had to be tough to be bombarded constantly.

"Yes, but after a while you get used to it, like water running off a duck's back," he replied in his enticing Scottish accent.

I can see why he was voted Sexiest Man Alive by People magazine when he was almost 60 years old. Upon hearing that news, he had commented, "Well there aren't many sexy dead men, are there?"

After his speech, I asked him to come up to the office of the National Press Club's president to pose for a picture. Walkie-talkies crackled back and forth as the security personnel and staff tried to locate the NPC president.

As we waited, Mr. and Mrs. Connery and I chatted about their life in the Bahamas. I found him to be a regular guy, more genuine than the movie image. After a short while, he asked if I needed him to do anything else before his next scheduled appearance. Trying to stall for time until NPC president Dick Ryan was reached, I kiddingly asked him if he wanted to pose with a few Press Club staffers and friends. He graciously took me up on it. We all cherish those pictures.

We finally got word that Ryan was at the Capitol on assignment. Each president of the club has to continue their job as a reporter while enjoying his or her one-year tenure as president. Then it was time for Mr. Connery to become "James Bond" again to pass through the throngs of admirers on the way back to his limo and on to his next engagement.

As I look back on my brief time with Secret Agent 007 holed up in the president's office, I marveled at his skill in responding to those who saw only a famous Hollywood spy. ✪

Chapter 13

My Three Presidents

**The White House
Jan. 16, 2010**

A YEAR AFTER President Bush left office, he returned to the Obama White House along with former President Clinton. They showed their support for the victims of the devastating earthquake in Haiti as they crossed parties in a united front for an all-American relief effort.

However, I had agreed to photograph a wedding for an acquaintance at 1 p.m. on that Saturday. At 11 p.m. the night before, I had received notice on the White House schedule that the past three, living, U.S. presidents would all speak in the Rose Garden — a rare press opportunity at the White House, or anywhere else for that matter. It was announced as a "pool only" event, with select members of the media granted access. It was risky for me to attend because I was not a part of the pool that day. I could only hope to get in. I had to try.

Logistics then came into play. Having covered each of those presidents, I was familiar with some of their habits. If they were late, I would be in big trouble because I was cutting my schedule very close if I wanted to get to that wedding.

Of the three, President Bush was the only one who was always punctual. I was betting that they would be on time but then again, the odds were against me. I began to obsess about the many details that would need to be in place.

For example, should I drive or take the metro? The timing was so close, my choices were critical. A simple traffic jam could derail me. I chose the metro and reasoned if the trains were delayed — as often happened on weekends — I could take a taxi as a backup plan. A repeated lesson I have learned over the years is always have a backup plan. As I arrived at the Northwest gate media entrance at the White House and stood among my fellow

EYES THAT SPEAK 75

Chapter 13 | My Three Presidents

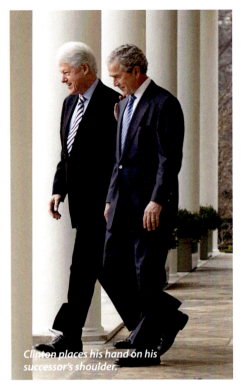

Clinton places his hand on his successor's shoulder.

Bush, Clinton and Obama unite.

Suddenly we heard the doors of the Oval Office fly open as the photographers who had a different angle on the other side of the Rose Garden began to fire off shots like it was the Wild West.

members of the press, I was greeted by the same Secret Service agents I saw regularly, yet they proceeded with extra caution as the bomb-sniffing dogs searched all our gear. "You are about to be standing within several yards of the most current three living U.S. presidents, so things are amped up around here," one of the agents informed us. This heightened my already soaring adrenaline as I looked at my watch, hoping for the best.

Standing in position, cameras aimed and ready, among the small group of photographers, I waited. Tick, tick, tick ... suddenly we heard the doors of the Oval Office fly open as the photographers who had a different angle on the other side of the Rose Garden began to fire off shots like it was the Wild West. The three leaders turned the corner, barreling toward us.

I cannot be sure, but I believe President Bush gave me a kind wink, as he had done many times over the years. As the presidents strode toward us, they turned and stepped between the white columns of the White House and into the Rose Garden to make remarks in support of the Haiti earthquake-relief efforts.

I barely heard their words as I kept an eye on the clock. However, I was aware of the camaraderie that was manifesting among the former leaders. Normally the media are not allowed to leave an event until the president has left the area. I prayed they would each be brief in their remarks.

Gratefully the event finished early, and I raced to the metro only to discover that my train was delayed. Moving instantly to plan B, I ran back to the street to hail a cab, but most of the cabbies refused to drive the 15 or so miles to Maryland. When I found a cooperative driver, I offered an additional $50 to his fare if he could get me home in 30 minutes. I mean to tell you that, that was one wild ride! I actually made it back to my home office in 25 minutes. I downloaded my pictures and got to the church five minutes early.

I have always been grateful that I took the gamble that day. Although enormously stressful, it was equally rewarding as I edited the pictures of the three presidents striding out of the Oval Office, exactly as I had envisioned it the night before in my fitful sleep. ✪

Chapter 14

Shaking Hands With Cool Hand Luke

I WAS PHOTOGRAPHING Gore Vidal, the famous author/playwright, at the National Press Club when I heard a rumor that a couple of "big shots" were in the audience. I decided that I would investigate after getting a few more close-ups of Vidal speaking at the podium.

Crawling through the room as I made my way to the head table, I found the perfect angle. I sat down on the floor but needed just a few inches to my right to get a clean shot. The only problem was a pair of black cowboy boots attached to outstretched legs were blocking my view. I leaned up alongside those boots to hint that I needed them to move over a few inches. No response. Finally, I tapped the boots and, looking up, whispered as I pointed to the owner's feet, "Excuse me, can you move your feet over just a few inches for me?" The piercing blue eyes looking at me were the legendary eyes of the renowned actor Paul Newman, aka "Cool Hand Luke."

He said, "Sure," and did just that. I held my position for a while with the realization that snagging Newman's picture would personally mean much more to me than procuring Gore Vidal's.

Throughout the remainder of Vidal's witty and entertaining speech, a wonderful, uninhibited laugh rose above the others in the audience. It was that of Joanne Woodward, Newman's wife, who was seated at another table. As the speech ended and we were off camera, the crowd began to mill around. I stood up and quickly found myself face-to-face with Paul Newman. I introduced myself to him as we shook hands and joked that all that time I was next to him, I did not aim my lens at him once. Then I asked if I could photograph him now. Smiling, he asked what I had in mind.

Deciding to go for it, I said it would be great if I could get a photograph of both him and his wife together. I sensed a certain shyness about him, and respecting that, did not want to overwhelm him by taking a lot of pictures. We talked as we waited for the love of his life, Joanne Woodward, to finish speaking with a few admirers. I asked him if he would consider coming to speak at the National Press Club someday.

He bashfully looked down and said softly, "No. I have nothing to say."

I mentioned that he had certainly accomplished a lot with his successful career and the generosity he showed with the contributions to charitable causes he made through his successful food enterprises. As we then spoke briefly about his racing interests, I looked around and noticed that there were more than a dozen people standing about 10 feet back, watching us. They just stared in disbelief that he happened to be in the audience.

As we continued to wait, I overheard a small part of a conversation between Joanne Woodward and a member of the audience. The woman told

Paul Newman
and Joanne Woodward
National Press Club
Washington, D.C.,
Oct. 5, 2002

Chapter 14 | Shaking Hands With Cool Hand Luke

Husband and wife actors Paul Newman and Joanne Woodward

The piercing blue eyes looking at me were the legendary eyes of the renowned actor Paul Newman, aka "Cool Hand Luke."

of her journey as an aspiring actress and said that she was now a member of the Screen Actors Guild. I was so impressed as I watched Woodward — this Oscar-winning actress — listen so attentively to a stranger's story and shower her with enthusiastic congratulations and encouragement. When they had finished talking, I introduced myself, shook hands with her and asked if I could photograph her and her husband. The famous duo cooperated, and we made small talk as I took my pictures, thanked them and we went our separate ways.

That legendary couple — both so friendly and cooperative — obviously loved, respected and deferred to each other. The chemistry between those two seasoned actors was more than obvious.

Still beaming from the glow of those two stars, I realized, even then, that unexpected photo op had provided a rare personal glimpse into this couple's real characters.

Chapter 15

Presidents, Protocol and Pageantry

STATE ARRIVALS CAN BE DRAMATIC, although usually quite predictable. There are several types of arrivals: the official working visit, official visit and the biggest — the official state visit. Each consisted of the president of the United States inviting and hosting another world leader.

Hundreds of staff members work well in advance of the official state visits to make them as seamless and effortless as possible.

A lot of "hurry up and wait" happens at these functions, which is a hallmark of this business. Most state arrival ceremonies take place at the South Portico, on the South Lawn of the White House, weather permitting. We typically need to

Trumpets sound at a White House state visit.

Presidential protective detail at their West Wing post and (left) Drum and Fife Corps performs at a state arrival ceremony.

gather at the Palm Room doors several hours ahead of starting time to compete for a good position during the preset process. Members of the pool get priority in selecting their positions.

Once the doors are opened and we are escorted by a White House staff member, a two- or three-story riser awaits us, each spot claimed by whomever gets there first. Imagine the competitive sprint that takes place among us, as most of us carry a stepladder in addition to our camera gear in this nonofficial race. Things tend to get a bit hectic as we hurry to secure a prime spot.

This is also when most of the scuffles occur. The preset process is very important, especially during any high-profile event. It is the best insurance one can have to make sure we each secure a prime position. Although we get along well with each other, it is when the members of the visiting press corps arrive and occasionally assert themselves, attempting to dominate, that there is a problem. In the event one of us misses the preset escort, that person is left to choose from the remaining, less desirable positions, unless a friend saves a spot with a small stepladder or camera bag.

continued on page 85

Queen Elizabeth II visits the White House during an official state arrival ceremony. Military in dress uniforms participated in the welcome festivities.

Chapter 15 | Presidents, Protocol and Pageantry

President Clinton and first lady Hillary welcome British Prime Minister Tony Blair and his wife, Cherie Blair, to the White House for a state dinner.

84   EYES THAT SPEAK

In the media world, photographers are referred to as "stills" (as in still-picture cameras) and the video network camera people are referred to as "sticks," because their heavier cameras generally require a tripod.

Exactly at the appointed time, with drums rolling, the U.S. president and first lady greet the guest head of state (and usually their spouse) as they emerge from their limo onto the red carpet. The U.S. president then walks the guest up onto the staging area for the playing of the national anthem from each country. Cannons fire off either a 19- or 21-gun salute. Representatives from all branches of the U.S. military stand at attention in their dress uniforms as the two world leaders strut by to review the troops, saluting them as they pass in front of the press risers, and then greet some of the hundreds of invited guests in the crowd.

Traditionally just a few photographers are allowed into what is known as the cutaway position (to the side of the stage). I have only been privileged to shoot from that area a handful of times during my career as a small news agency. The majority of both foreign and national press corps shoot these events from the "head on" position, which is farther away but still has the White House in the background.

The precision of the military stance and perfection of the dress uniforms offer some nice, photographic opportunities. In the past, Presidents Clinton, Bush and Obama included a well-choreographed photo op of the two first couples waving from the South Portico balcony.

Quite often, in past administrations, we would be privileged to have a photo op with the guest head of state and the U.S. president sitting side by side in the Oval Office chatting and shaking hands.

continued on page 88

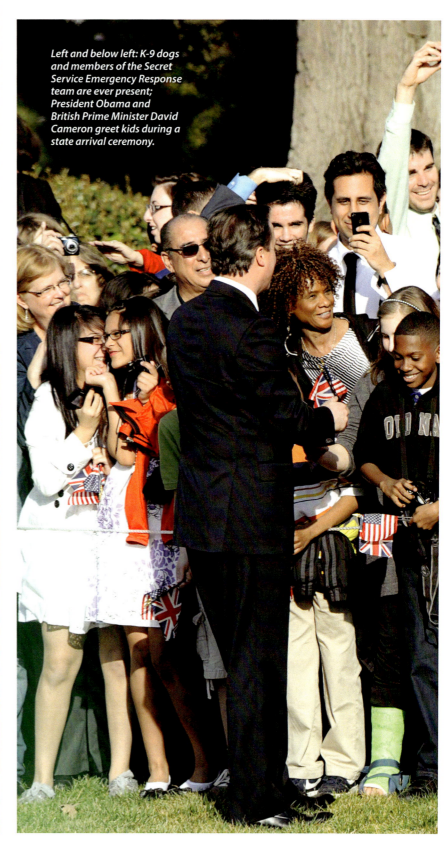

Left and below left: K-9 dogs and members of the Secret Service Emergency Response team are ever present; President Obama and British Prime Minister David Cameron greet kids during a state arrival ceremony.

86 EYES THAT SPEAK

Chapter 15 | Presidents, Protocol and Pageantry

Top: President Obama and first lady Michelle welcome President Xi and Madame Peng Liyuan of China to the White House during an official state visit on the South Lawn.
Above: Presidents Trump and Macron share a candid moment.
Opposite: The leaders review the troops during a state arrival ceremony at the White House.

Normally that was a 10- to 20-second window for those of us in the expanded pool unless the leaders took a couple of questions from reporters.

The White House usually hosts a lunch in either the private residence or the smaller dining room on the State Floor. Afterward, the two principals would often hold a joint press conference. This is generally what we call a "two and two" among the media, as each leader answers two questions from American reporters and two from the foreign visiting press.

Meanwhile, the first ladies normally do something locally, such as visiting an area of interest. They may pay a call to an educational facility or a performing arts school. Sometimes, the first ladies may simply share a private cup of tea and conversation in the Yellow Oval Room. This routine is subject to each administration's style, because every U.S. president puts his own thumbprint onto the state arrival scenario.

I continue to always look for some type of natural moment during those events, such as the momentary pause with Presidents Donald Trump and Emmanuel Macron of France during a press conference or the president leaning in to give the first lady a kiss as they hosted their first state arrival ceremony.

Typically, a formal State Dinner is hosted by the U.S. president on the State Floor of the White House, peppered with prominent members of society, entertainers and government officials. There are two types of dinners: state and official, determined by strict protocol. The chief of protocol from the State Department, the White House chief usher and the White House social secretary oversee the planning from start to finish.

State Dinners are usually black- or

white-tie events held in honor of kings, queens or heads of government. Again, early arrival for the press is recommended. Typically, at 6:59 p.m., the president and first lady emerge from the North Portico to greet the honored occupants at their limousine at exactly 7 p.m. This means a photographer must get a place in the lineup by 5 p.m. or earlier to secure a good spot.

Members of the media must request to cover either the arrival of the visiting first couple or the arrival of the guests at the dinner. Inside the front door of the State Floor of the White House, the receiving line is generally photographed by the president's personal photographers as well as by the "tight pool," consisting of the wire and major news organizations. After the arrivals, selected members of the media are allowed to briefly photograph the champagne toast prior to dinner.

In total, covering a state arrival day is approximately 15 hours long including editing and transmission of pictures. The actual shooting time is only about 90 minutes, tops. ✺

Chapter 15 | Presidents, Protocol and Pageantry

Above: President Trump leans in to kiss his wife, Melania, during a state arrival ceremony for President Emmanuel Macron of France.

Right: President Trump and first lady Melania welcome His Majesty King Abdullah II and Queen Rania of Jordan to the White House.

Chapter 15 | Presidents, Protocol and Pageantry

German Chancellor Angela Merkel and President Trump at the closing of a two and two press conference.

Left: First lady Melania Trump and first lady Juliana Awada of Argentina walk along the Colonnade to the Oval Office.

President Donald Trump welcomes President Muhammadu Buhari of the Federal Republic of Nigeria to the White House.

Chapter 16

Mother Teresa
Saintly Warrior

MOTHER TERESA WAS a public figure by whom I had always been intrigued. I loved the way she was not afraid to get down and dirty, whether with royalty, heads of state or homeless people. Her work ranged from starting open-air classrooms for the poor children of Kolkata, to beginning her own order of nuns, the Missionaries of Charity. The sisters' primary purpose was to love and care for the sick, dying and forgotten of the poorest of the poor all around the world. It seems like these words of Kent M. Keith were found written on the wall of Mother Teresa's home for children in Kolkata. I think this expresses her outlook in life.

"People are often unreasonable and self-centered
FORGIVE THEM ANYWAY

If you are kind, people may accuse you of ulterior motives
BE KIND ANYWAY

If you are honest, people may cheat you
BE HONEST ANYWAY

If you find happiness, people may be jealous
BE HAPPY ANYWAY

The good you do today may be forgotten
DO GOOD ANYWAY

Give the world your best and it may never be enough
GIVE YOUR BEST ANYWAY

For you see, in the end it is between
YOU AND GOD
It was never between you and them anyway."

St. John the Baptist Catholic Church
Silver Spring, MD,
May 31, 1996

Mother Teresa greets Maureen Dalton.

To me, that woman was a true warrior. She had long since been on my bucket list of superstars I had hoped to photograph someday.

While in Kathmandu, I decided to take a quick hop over to Kolkata, since I was in the neighborhood anyway, and scout out Mother Teresa. However, word on the street was that she was actually in the Washington, D.C., area. Imagine my surprise when I returned home and found she had been only a couple of miles from where I lived! As it turned out, we passed each other flying to opposite sides of the world. Several times I heard that Mother Teresa was in this area, and it was always after the fact that I learned of her visit and then poof! She was gone ... elusive, just like the Lone Ranger.

Later, I was thrilled upon learning from a friend that she would be just a few miles from me in Silver Spring, Maryland, in a couple of weeks. It was great to finally have some advance notice. The purpose of her trip was to witness the final vows of her novice sisters at a local church. At last, it seemed I had a chance to capture that amazing woman on film.

The morning she was to arrive, I was there early and slowly beginning to establish a friendly relationship with the protective detail officials. I find this is always a good idea because security personnel can either help or prevent you from getting a decent picture. Eventually I learned the itinerary for her arrival from those same security guys. It seemed she was arriving by bus with the soon-to-be nuns and was scheduled only to wave at the crowd of parishioners and neighbors who had gotten wind of her visit. That inside info helped me select my stakeout position for the best angle.

After a short while, I called the friends who had tipped me off about this event because they lived close by. I let them know that I was able to secure a prime viewing spot for them if they could make it. It wasn't long before my two friends and their daughter, Maureen, arrived, carrying a small camping stool as we all waited for Mother Teresa to arrive. Maureen has been chronically ill since she was a baby and is one of the bravest people I know. She has continued to baffle and amaze doctors for the past several decades with her resilience and shining personality in the face of severe, ongoing medical challenges. Although Maureen has several limitations including her physical inability to stand for any length of time, she always has a cheerful attitude and a hearty handshake to offer anyone she meets.

That signature trait of hers radiated like a beacon to Mother Teresa and the small nun who had begun to walk along the designated path, suddenly veered off course and made a beeline to Maureen. Although I knew Maureen's hefty handshake awaited her, I was surprised when Mother Teresa was the first to reach for Maureen's hand. As she leaned down to look into her eyes, she gently said, "I know many like you."

Maureen responded with a jovial, "Hi, Mother Teresa!" as if they were old friends. Mother Teresa continued to talk with Maureen softly, the two of them seemingly in their own world as I took pictures, until a man whisked in to take her away to keep her on schedule. Before leaving, however, she shook hands with Maureen's parents, and as she reached out for my hand, that same man abruptly stepped between us, blocking our contact. Apparently noticing my disappointment, Mother Teresa managed to slip back behind him and took my hand in hers. I vividly remember how soft her hands were. With all of the hard, physical work she did, I had expected them to be rough and calloused.

That small gesture of hers meant a lot to me. She gave me a smile and a moment of special recognition — I assume — for capturing that moment between my friend Maureen and herself.

I went into that day seemingly setting up an opportunity to get a few pictures but ended up with an intimate photo op thanks to Maureen. If I learned a lesson, I came to realize that what the world considers to be a disability, on the grander scale, may be truly extraordinary.

Chapter 17

One More for "The Gipper"

Former President Ronald Reagan's funeral procession to the U.S. Capitol.

THE FUNERAL OF former President Ronald Reagan was the first state funeral I had ever covered, and I was stunned to see the amount of planning that had been invested so many years in advance. I was not aware that sitting U.S. presidents planned their own funerals upon first getting into office. That was particularly elaborate, possibly due to his time spent in Hollywood prior to his life in politics. He had been an actor, especially known for his portrayal of "The Gipper," a famous Notre Dame quarterback. The summary of all his roles came together as we celebrated his long, diverse life.

June 2004 was unseasonably hot. Both the media and onlookers waited in

**Ronald Reagan State Funeral
Washington, D.C.,
June 11, 2004**

oppressive heat to see the procession along the winding route to the U.S. Capitol. We vigilantly monitored the parade route for any sign or word of arrival in our vicinity. The streets were set up with barricades confining tens of thousands of patriotic Americans determined to witness the pageantry and say farewell to a beloved leader.

A disaster almost happened when the small, misguided aircraft of a U.S. Midwestern governor unknowingly entered

continued on page 98

Chapter 17 | One More for "The Gipper"

As the horse-drawn presidential caisson arrives at the Capitol, a member of the honor guard passes out from the heat.

America pays its respects to former President Reagan at the U.S. Capitol.

Nancy Reagan made sure that her husband had been honored in the same grand fashion that she had loved him.

EYES THAT SPEAK

Chapter 17 | One More for "The Gipper"

the restricted airspace around the U.S. Capitol. That led to the evacuation of the Capitol and the surrounding area in record time according to House Speaker Dennis Hastert.

We were instructed by the police to move out of the area immediately, abandon our gear and go toward Union Station. People stampeded in a frantic effort to survive what was thought to be another terrorist attack.

That evacuation caused us to forfeit the hard-earned positions along the route that we had secured six to 10 hours in advance. After the plane was successfully escorted away by military aircraft, we received an "all clear" signal and scrambled to reclaim our original vantage points.

Finally, the parade of various military groups in dress uniform, along with the Marine Corps band, marched by with the formal precision you would expect of an event of this magnitude. The officers keeping guard along the parade route stood at attention in the heat for such a long period that some even fainted and were instantly carried off and replaced by another. Off in the distance, the clip-clop of horse hooves could be heard, and as the echoing sound got louder and tension mounted, an eerie silence fell over the sea of bystanders as the flag-wrapped casket ceremoniously passed us by.

Once we were inside the Capitol, the presidential viewing procedures fell into place. Military were vigilantly protecting the casket and stood on ceremony, changing the guard every 15 minutes. A procession quickly formed, with thousands of citizens awaiting their turn to pay their respects at the 24-hour viewing. Periodically, the line was interrupted as various heads of state and members of Congress cut in with their official escorts.

The following day I covered the ceremony at the National Cathedral.

The military's final salute to their former commander in chief.

The former first lady Nancy Reagan is escorted to the National Cathedral.

The funeral motorcade made its way down the streets of Washington, D.C., which were lined with crowds of people. The hallowed building was the last stop for many dignitaries. There, inside the carefully secured grounds, was a crowd of celebrities, royalty and various heads of state. A frail Nancy Reagan emerged from a limousine, accompanied by military escort, and wound her way into the towering cathedral.

As we waited for the end of the service, leaders from the different branches of the U.S. military lined up and stood at attention to salute the casket as it was brought out to the awaiting presidential hearse.

Looking back on that, I see what an enormous love story Ronald and Nancy Reagan lived. That funeral was so much more than our nation losing a former leader. The Reagans' fairy tale relationship played out publicly. Nancy and her husband had shared a profound love for each other, and the world witnessed their farewell. Other than my own parents, who were married for 65 years, I have never witnessed such a powerful union. Nancy Reagan made sure that her husband had been honored in the same grand fashion that she had loved him. Someone once quoted her as saying that the word love was not big enough to describe what they had together.

As the huge motorcade left the cathedral, everyone was moved. For the Reagan family, however, there was much more to come, as they headed to California for more services that would continue to honor President Reagan's memory, and to execute the final wishes and vision he and Nancy had planned so many years ago. As she said her final goodbye, the honor guard gave one last salute to "The Gipper." ✪

Chapter 18

Hijinx With Holiness

Pope John Paul II
Oct. 8, 1995

DURING MY photography career, I have had the honor of photographing three different popes when they had visited the Washington, D.C., area. Each pontiff's visit was as unique as their widely different personalities.

I had received word that Pope John Paul II was coming to Maryland, and as a newly accredited member of the media, I was stoked at the opportunity to cover a world-famous figure. I quickly learned that having credentials did not guarantee me access. I spoke to my bureau chief, Sarah McClendon, who unconditionally supported me in my mission to cover the Holy Father's arrival. Although Sarah was not personally covering that event, she allowed me to represent her news service. She was gracious enough to sponsor my sister, Cathy, who was a very devout Catholic.

We then made the trip to Baltimore, along with a seasoned tabloid photographer friend who had been helping me navigate with my newly acquired credentials. As we waited to check in, I was overjoyed to see only three people in line. Unfortunately, one of the three journalists was from ABC News and picking up hundreds of credentials at once. Hours later, it was finally my turn.

We were told that the pope would visit three venues in Baltimore, and we would need a credential for each: the arrival at the Baltimore airport, the Mass at Camden Yards Stadium and along the parade route. We were instructed that we could not cover two events back-to-back because it would be impossible to get from one location to the next in time.

During this process, I met a nun who regaled us with her story of the pope's

Pope John Paul II

**Pope John Paul II
Arrival at
BWI Airport
Baltimore, MD,
Oct. 8, 1995**

EYES THAT SPEAK 101

Chapter 18 | Hijinx With Holiness

prior visit. She said that she had worked at the World Youth Mass when the pope had visited Colorado years earlier. She was among those chosen to distribute communion, and she said they had been instructed to stop after five minutes for scheduling purposes, no matter what. They all had known there would be many disappointments in the crowd but were resolved to keep to the schedule.

She said that everyone received communion in under three minutes, with time to spare. I was struck by the volume of pious people, some even in religious garb, looking for credentials and even willing to say or do anything to get the coveted passes.

At long last, we finally received our passes. The tabloid photographer did not receive one, but he was gracious enough to lend me his 600mm lens. He pointed out that it was worth $10,000, and if I dropped it, I would need to sign over the title of my car to him. That lens was so huge that I needed my tripod. Although appreciative of his gesture, I was still worried that he could be driving off with my car at the end of the day.

On the morning of the pope's arrival, we had to be at the cargo area of BWI airport before 5 a.m. for screening and securing our position on the risers. Each news agency was assigned its vantage point, and McClendon News Service, a small news bureau, was appointed a mediocre position. But we were inside the press area, and that was what mattered most.

As we were waiting for the pope, I was able to assume a vacant Newsweek slot. I asked one of the plain-clothes officers how much longer our wait would be, and after a few minutes, he informed me in a monotone fashion, "Shepherd One is now wheels-up in Philadelphia."

Translation: The pope's aircraft, named Shepherd One, had just taken off and it would be 45 minutes or so before we saw the plane. I have since learned that the pope does not have his own plane but flies privately on various airlines. Air Force One is the call sign for our U.S. president; Shepherd One is the international call sign of any aircraft with the pope on board. Eventually, we saw

Some folks walk away with cherished items, some with precious intangibles and others with nothing at all.

a small dot on the horizon come into view as the aircraft drew nearer.

Shortly after the white-and-red Trans World aircraft landed, cardinals wearing their signature red and black began disembarking the plane. One after another they descended the stairs. At last, a blast of white appeared in the doorway of the aircraft, and there stood Pope John Paul II, blessing the crowd with a sweeping sign of the cross to the left, right and center before heading down the stairs. He was quickly engulfed by the waiting crowd and swallowed up from my view.

As my sister, Cathy, and I walked away from the media area, I hoped to have captured a nice shot of His Holiness, so I carefully made my way to the car with the huge, borrowed lens. I was relieved that all had gone well. As we passed a small reporters' shuttle bus destined for the parade route, Cathy turned to me and said she had to get to that Mass. We talked to the bus driver, who insisted that he was not allowed to make any stops before the destination ... the parade route. We asked whether she could just get off close to the stadium at a red light. She flashed him one of her big smiles and he reluctantly agreed. As the bus approached Camden Yards, the other reporters shouted, "Get off now!" My sister's wishes had been fulfilled as she gained entry into the stadium, attended Mass and received communion from the pope and then managed, hours later, to find a train to take her home.

Two decades later, Pope John Paul II was declared a saint by the Catholic Church.

Looking back on that experience, it seemed that although thousands of us witnessed Pope John Paul II's visit, our individual reasons for coming determined what we took away from the day. As a photojournalist, I took the defining picture of John Paul II blessing the crowd and commemorating his visit for history. My sister was able to see her spiritual leader. However, the paparazzi left empty-handed. It seems that this phenomenon holds true for a lot of things in life. Some folks walk away with cherished items, some with precious intangibles and others with nothing at all.

Pope Benedict XVI
April 16, 2008

Pope Benedict XVI in the Oval Office.

THE NEXT TIME I encountered a pope, it was Benedict XVI on his visit to the White House. This time, I was fortunate enough to be a member of the White House Press Corps, with proper credentials. The White House Press Office told us that April 15 was the pope's birthday, and maybe his visit would only be a quiet lunch with President Bush, maybe not.

I was anxious to put my White House Press Pass to use, so I eagerly awaited the event. The word among the Press Corps was that the window for credentials of visiting press was limited. I was so grateful that I obtained guaranteed access this time. Unlike during John Paul II's visit, a limited number of media could cover this event inside the gates of the White House. That was a wonderful opportunity for the photogs at the White House. Fewer photographers meant that the pictures would be more valuable.

A huge number of cardinals and bishops paraded past the media as we waited for an escort to the area where we would each claim our position. During the clergy procession, several of them seemed to look at us with apprehension.

Meanwhile, outside the White House, a crowd had been gathering since the night before with the hopes of catching a glimpse of the pope-mobile carrying what we had begun calling him: B-16 — Pope Benedict XVI. They were all

> **The White House**
> Washington, D.C.,
> April 16, 2008

chanting, singing and carrying religious signs, a few in protest. There was a rumor that there were two motorcades bearing the pope, the first carrying a "fake pope," who was a decoy for the real pope, who was to follow soon after and enter the White House.

When Pope Benedict finally arrived at 1600 Pennsylvania Ave., we were ready for him. This time I had a loaner 400mm 2.8 lens from Nikon Professional Services. This lens was huge but well worth the inconvenience of its size because of the crisp images it produced. As the pope emerged from his limo, he did the customary blessing of the crowd, as I had witnessed in Baltimore by Pope John Paul II.

President Bush and first lady Laura greeted Pope Benedict warmly, and we proceeded with the customary state arrival ceremony I had come to know so well.

Traditionally, members of each branch of the military waited at attention in dress uniform as the troops were reviewed. Instead of the usual branches of military in dress uniforms, a select group of Boy and Girl Scouts stood at attention. A few passed out from the heat and maybe from the stress of the event. I am sure it was a big honor to be one of the chosen few selected for this ceremony.

Following the welcoming remarks from both President Bush and Pope Benedict, we were advised — at the last minute — that both would be walking along the Colonnade to the Oval Office. If we were to get a photo opportunity, we had to move NOW! Grabbing my heavy gear and stepladder, I rushed down the stairs of the riser and quickly staked out my spot in the Rose Garden, seconds before our two subjects emerged from the Palm Room.

The president and pope walked along, chatting casually as they drifted from

Pope Benedict XVI tours the White House.

shadows to bright sunlight. The pope, dressed in bright white, challenged the most seasoned of professional photographers as our meter readings soared up and down, struggling with this difficult lighting situation.

Once they entered the Oval Office, we moved from behind the red velvet ropes and into place at the holding area, waiting for the White House Press Office wranglers to signal us to come in for a 10- to 20-second photo op.

This wait can normally be anywhere from five minutes to one hour long. We were divided into several waves of around 12 photographers each since there were a lot of overseas press. I had decided that I

EYES THAT SPEAK **105**

Chapter 18 | Hijinx With Holiness

President Bush meets with Pope Benedict XVI in the Oval Office.

needed to be in the first wave while both subjects were still "fresh" and not impatient with us yet.

Many things ran through my mind as I changed my camera settings while briskly walking toward the Oval Office. I set my second camera for the proper exposure that I was accustomed to using in the Oval Office, guessing on the adjustments for this rare picture of Pope Benedict as he sat with his white robes radiating, altering my familiar calculations.

Surprisingly, when getting to the holding position on the Colonnade, I did not have to even pause because the White House press handler immediately ushered me around the corner and into the Oval Office. Since I had been the first photographer in line to arrive, I stood directly in front of the pope, seated next to President Bush in the customary two chairs in front of the fireplace. Normally, as photographers, we are not to speak unless spoken to first.

Seizing the couple of seconds while I was the only photographer from the Press Corps, I said, "Hi, Your Holiness. Welcome to Washington." President Bush smiled at me while the pope looked into my eyes for a brief instant, as if about to speak but then gazed with astonishment over my shoulder at my fellow photographers, scrambling behind me then, as they burst into the room. In all of my years covering the White House, I can never recall being the first of the pack to enter the Oval Office for a photo. The pope silently blessed us, making the sign of the cross while we finished taking our pictures. As we were escorted out of the room, I realized I came away with more than I had hoped for that day.

As I walked out of the White House compound, I was absorbed back into the crowd of thousands who waited for a glimpse of His Holiness. I made my way home to Bethesda, Maryland, to transmit pictures to my agency. A short time later, I was scheduled to photograph the pope again at the Vatican Embassy for Our Lady of Lourdes School (my alma mater).

I stood outside the Vatican Embassy with a few hundred parishioners, once again jockeying for position — this time with nonmedia, waving their cellphones and small cameras, eagerly awaiting their chance to see the pope. At last, when His Holiness finally did emerge, I had only been able to get a couple of decent pictures of him, but that was okay. I had already had my chance, and it was time for others to have their own opportunity and story to tell.

Pope Francis
Sept. 23, 2015

POPE FRANCIS WAS THE third pope that I had photographed. The security was much greater than my other experiences, and media availability was limited, especially at the White House. None of the working press knew if we were even going to be able to have access to cover the pope's visit with the president until a few days prior. Members of the media were required to RSVP to the White House announcement of the state arrival during a very brief window. Luckily, I responded in time, gratefully receiving a final email confirmation.

I once again had to be in place before the trains started running because the roads would be closed off to allow traffic to get downtown. Strategic, logistical planning was once again called into action.

I arrived a little after 4:30 a.m. and there was already a large crowd of media waiting for the checkpoint to open. After getting cleared in, I went around to the usual waiting area outside of the White House Palm Room for the official escort to preset our positions.

I expected to see the normal group of photographers and other media, but no one was there. I asked the Secret Service agent in the booth where everyone was. He said, "They just went out; go ahead through the doors and catch up with them."

Members of the press are not allowed through the Palm Room doors without an escort from a staffer from the Lower Press Office. I figured everyone was just

**Washington, D.C.,
Sept. 23-24, 2015**

The White House
Press Office
1600 Pennsylvania Avenue, NW
Washington, DC 20500

September 23, 2015

Folks,

You should have received this information last week, and I've been in touch with a lot of you confirming who from your organization is credentialed. Here's a reminder of the access restrictions:

<u>NO access to the White House before 5:00AM</u>.
6:15AM - Final call for any press with camera equipment Pennsylvania Avenue. <u>NO cameras will be processed after 6:15AM.</u>
7:15AM – Final call for press without camera equipment to arrive Pennsylvania Avenue. <u>There is NO access to the White House from 7:15AM until the Pope has left the White House, scheduled for approximately 11:00AM</u>.

Get here as early as possible. <u>If you don't process through security before these times and they close these gates, I HAVE NO ABILITY TO GET YOU INTO THE COMPLEX</u>. Zero – can't help you. There's an 11th temporary Commandment in place just for tomorrow that everyone will follow, and it's "Thou shalt not arrive late as thou shalt not be able to make it onto the White House complex." I cannot stress that enough. Get here early.

This is all the information I have for you. I legitimately do not have the bandwidth to answer any specific question except if you need clarity on who from your organization is credentialed.

<u>I have zero information about the parade or anything for the visit that doesn't happen between 5AM and 11AM Wednesday on White House grounds, so don't bother asking me for details."</u>

---

a couple of yards ahead, took his advice and proceeded through the doors. Camera crews were already set up on the risers that were in place on the South Lawn. I discovered there was an unusually small area far away for still photographers. Our platform was deserted. I looked around to see the "Good Morning America" camera crew setting up, and all the other morning talk shows were doing live broadcasts from the White House South Lawn.

I quickly staked out one of the limited spots for myself and my two fellow photographer friends, leaving behind a small stool, camera bag and monopod to secure our positions. Knowing protocol, I then searched for a White House escort to guide me back to the holding area where the rest of the press would be gathering. It was important that I not remain in a premier position when the rest of the press photographers were escorted out to the

Chapter 18 | Hijinx With Holiness

The president and first lady receive Pope Francis at the White House.

The smallest of gestures would mean "surrender" in the claim for a place in line.

South Lawn for preset. I would have been in big trouble with the White House pool and wire service photographers for getting a jump on everyone else and marking my spot.

I found an escort back to the Palm Room, where we all patiently stood for more than an hour, so I could be escorted back to my already staked-out position. A very tall, well-known, magazine photographer jumped in front of me. He and I stood toe-to-toe for at least another half hour as we each held firm to battle for our positions. The smallest of gestures would mean "surrender" in the claim for a place in line. He eventually relinquished his place, loudly criticizing me for being aggressive and stating that there was plenty of room out on the South Lawn riser for all of us. I knew otherwise but could not let on.

As the doors finally opened and everyone rushed to the small riser that would not accommodate us all, I was behind in the scramble to grab a spot on the shrunken platform. I was, however, confident that I had already secured a spot for me and my friends. One friend, however, did not get there fast enough and lost the position I had saved for him.

Another hour or so later, the pope finally arrived. As he got out of his humble Fiat, the first lady seemed to be surprised, although most of us did not have a clear path to get that picture.

As the sun began to rise on the horizon, a photographer's nightmare unfolded. Pope Francis stood up, and his white robe was luminescent in the sunlight before the bright white of the White House. President Obama, wearing a dark suit, stood in the shadows of the stage.

Chapter 18 | Hijinx With Holiness

Pope Francis addresses the U.S. Congress along with members of the Supreme Court.

Unfortunately, the sun had shifted dramatically, and I was challenged to get a decent photo during a lot of the ceremony. Finally, the three moved up to the Truman Balcony where the even lighting finally shined down on the president, first lady and pope as they waved to the crowd.

Sept. 24, 2015, the next day, I photographed the pope giving his address to Congress. The occasion would be a first in history. Press photographers were required to have a letter of assignment from a magazine or newspaper in order to even cover Pope Francis' address before Congress.

Once again, we all had to arrive many hours early to secure our assigned positions. I was thankful to get a spot inside the Capitol where the pope was speaking. The members of Congress were reminded not to reach out and touch the pope as he entered the chambers. Members of the press were instructed that the format was the same as the State of the Union address.

Chapter 18 | Hijinx With Holiness

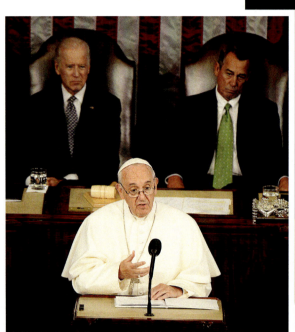

Pope Francis captivates Congress.

We were told the pope would walk down the aisle with hands folded in a prayer position to discourage members of Congress from trying to shake hands with him.

I was very impressed that Pope Francis had spoken from printed notes, both at the White House and before Congress, in English. His remarks were on point and well received.

The pope had been invited to lunch with the members of Congress but declined, choosing to spend it with some of the homeless people of Washington, D.C., bringing alive his own words, "Be poor among the poor. We need to include the excluded and preach peace."

I was able to watch his departure from inside the Capitol as the little Fiat, surrounded by a legion of large black SUVs, wound its way back to "his people."

Chapter 19

Old-World Charm

I HAD SPENT THE day photographing President Viktor Yushchenko of Ukraine. He was the political rock star of the hour at that time. He unknowingly drank poisonous soup in an assassination attempt in late 2004. Reports confirmed he had ingested hazardous amounts of TCDD, the most potent dioxin and a contaminant in Agent Orange. His handsome face had become scarred and shriveled. Yet that setback did not stop him from delivering his message to the Ukrainian people and the world. That man had the support of his people in a big way.

Unlike his opponent, he and his followers wanted Ukraine to be a democratic state, independent of Russia. The same followers camped out in the streets peacefully for 17 days to support Yushchenko. That became known as the "Orange Revolution" because they had donned the color again, 500,000 strong, to lobby for his election.

President Yushchenko was soon on his worldwide tour and headed for Washington, D.C. I photographed him during his visit with President Bush at the White House. That was a working visit, which included a photo op in the Oval Office along with a joint press conference. I never heard him speak English during those events.

Later that day I was to photograph Yushchenko again. This time, I was shooting for the Democratic National Committee who was hosting an event in his honor at the Willard Hotel. I was issued a special pin that allowed me access to the VIP green room — the holding area that was set up for all the dignitaries to enjoy wine and appetizers and relax until they went onstage. I was fortunate enough to witness some wonderfully candid moments among some of the key players in our diplomatic world as we waited for President Yushchenko. Former Secretary of State Madeleine Albright chatted away with former President Vaclav Havel of the Czech Republic — anti-Communist dissident

President Viktor Yushchenko
The Willard Hotel
Washington, D.C.,
April 7, 2005

EYES THAT SPEAK 113

Chapter 19 | Old-World Charm

> **I think it is safe to say it is unlikely that another world leader will ever be bowing and kissing my hand again. However, I will remember that for a brief moment I, too, felt honored.**

A healthier President Yushchenko returns to Washington, D.C., in September 2008.

and playwright — in what appeared to be his native language. Albright and Havel took to the flag-filled stage and engaged the cheering crowd with polished remarks, stalling until Yushchenko's arrival.

When Yushchenko finally appeared, a thunderous burst of applause echoed throughout the large ballroom as he was escorted onto the stage. It was there, through a translator, he told of his struggles and dreams for the future of Ukraine.

After his speech, he went briefly back to the green room, where Madeleine Albright presented him with a large coffee-table book documenting the Orange Revolution with a large centerfold picture of his victorious election. He smiled as he looked at this unique gift, and considerately moved slightly to one side for me so I could get a better angle of him with President Havel and Madeleine Albright.

I was so inspired by the courage this man had shown in his remarks throughout the day, continuing to voice his message no matter what the consequences. I was also impressed by his kindness to me in the midst of such excitement.

As he made his way to the door, surrounded by both Ukrainian security and U.S. protective detail, I reached out to him and said, "Thank you, Mr. President." To my amazement he turned to me, bowed, took my hand and kissed it, thanking me in perfect English for photographing him!

I looked around to see if anyone had, by chance, photographed that exchange, but of course no one had. Unfortunately, his personal photographer was 20 or so people away in the crowd. That was one of the rare times I regretted being the only official photographer.

I think it is safe to say it is unlikely that another world leader will ever be bowing and kissing my hand again. However, I will remember that for a brief moment I, too, felt honored.

Sometime later, when I next photographed President Yushchenko, I was happy to see that his health had improved. ✺

Chapter 20

President Barack Obama

EYES THAT SPEAK 115

Barack Obama | Code Name: Renegade
January 2009-2017

ONCE UPON A TIME, there was a young senator from Chicago. No one had heard much about the new kid on the block. He was a shooting star that rose above the other candidates and went on to become the first African American president of the United States.

Barack Obama's inauguration was the most historic of the five that I had photographed. Because Obama was the first African American U.S. president, his inauguration was a landmark. The atmosphere was one of pride and eloquence, a declaration of the future and an acknowledgment of the past, so from my vantage point, more than history was in the air.

I applied for my special Capitol Hill credentials, which would have hopefully allowed me to be top-drawer in the front row. Originally, I was turned down with a formal letter that my application for an inaugural press pass was denied because credentials were being sought from around the world, with a limited number of positions. After several conversations with God, the late Sarah McClendon (my patron saint of news emergencies) and the Senate Press Photographers Gallery, I let destiny take its course.

It was just a few days before the ceremony that I was informed that I had secured a position for the inauguration. I will be forever grateful for the opportunity to capture that moment in history. When I went to pick up my coveted credentials and saw the superb position that I was assigned, I was elated.

I was told that clearance onto the

A young Senator Barack Obama reviews his notes before speaking.

Overview of Barack Obama's renowned first inauguration

Capitol grounds would be between 4 a.m. and 6 a.m. Once again, how would I get there? Everywhere around the Capitol was closed for security. The metro trains were opening early, but in my neighborhood the first train to arrive was full. I made up my mind that there was no way that train was leaving without me. I squeezed on, knowing that, before the sun had risen, the day was boding well for the country and maybe even for me.

As I arrived at the Capitol, it was hard to recognize my fellow members of the media because almost everyone was bundled up to combat the brutally cold weather. Finally, I was inside the temporary trailer that housed the metal detectors that scanned each of us and our equipment. Secure in the knowledge that my position was safely reserved and marked with tape, I decided to go exploring. After a few hours, I noticed one of my fellow photographers coming out of a dark corridor and decided to investigate.

There were two heated, flushing bathrooms, along with an old, half-collapsed, leather couch stashed in a corner. Eureka! I knew from covering previous inaugurations what a gold mine that was. When covering a long, freezing-cold event like that, it was much like camping.

After a while, I decided to make sure no one was encroaching on the piece of tape that marked my position. It was important to stand in place so that no poachers could creep over into my 12-inch area because just a few inches can sometimes make a big difference, especially for an event of that magnitude.

In revisiting my spot and introducing myself to my neighbors, I was basically marking my territory. The Capitol grounds then began stirring to life as the thousands of empty chairs were slowly being filled. I decided to keep roaming around to stay warm and observe how the event was coming together.

I found one of my photog buddies, and

EYES THAT SPEAK   117

Chapter 20 | President Barack Obama

As the president-elect takes the oath of office ...

he realizes a mistake is being made.

In several seconds, this historic moment would be gone forever, with or without me.

together we wandered around to keep warm, finally ending up in a heated trailer that housed one of the larger networks where we enjoyed hot cocoa and a bagel and came away with a new pair of hand warmers, totally refreshed.

As the sun came up, it was fascinating to watch the landscape transform into a backdrop for millions of people from all parts of the world, thrilled to witness history as it unfolded before their eyes.

Finally, it was time to get into position. I was concerned that the president-elect might be blocked from our view because once the swearing in began, we would be standing behind Supreme Court Chief Justice John Roberts, who would be administering the oath of office. As a backup, I scoped out a second and third emergency vantage point on our riser just in case. Vice President Joe Biden was sworn in first and I had a wonderful

position. Justice John Paul Stevens, who swore in Vice President Biden, was much shorter than Chief Justice Roberts. Sure enough, when they got in position for the swearing in of President Barack Obama, from where I stood, he was completely blocked with the exception of his right ear. I was in a panic!

In several seconds, this historic moment would be gone forever, with or without me. Moving faster than I ever

Nine months after taking office, President Obama learns he has won the Nobel Peace Prize.

Chapter 20 | President Barack Obama

President Obama signs the Affordable Care Act.

realized was possible, I gently catapulted to my plan B position, careful not to shake the riser for the sake of the TV networks.

Then I opened fire with my trusty Nikon, and I prayed that the battery in my camera would not freeze up again, as it had earlier. In the back of my mind, I felt like something was wrong, but I could not identify it. As it turned out, Chief Justice Roberts had spoken a couple of the words of the oath out of order. Obama recognized it immediately but continued on to avoid embarrassing him (at least that was my impression).

Moving back to my assigned position, I found that my fellow photographer was inconsolable. "I was completely blocked! I have nothing!" My heart went out to him. It is always a disappointment for any of us when we walk away from a big moment without getting what we came for. This experience proved to me, once again, that it is always a good idea to have a backup plan. So, this lesson is the same as the one that I learned from my skydiving training. Always be aware of that emergency rip cord, because sometimes, you just don't get a second chance.

Obama swears in a second time as his family looks on.

Eight months later, I received a breaking news bulletin that newly-elected President Barack Obama had just won the Nobel Peace Prize for his extraordinary efforts to strengthen international diplomacy and cooperation between peoples. Members of the White House Press Corps rushed to the Rose Garden, and after a long delay, President Obama

EYES THAT SPEAK 121

Presidents Clinton and Obama joke around; Vice President Biden and Speaker John Boehner share a friendly moment.

emerged from the Oval Office with what I considered to be an "aw-shucks" kind of demeanor.

He humbly stated, "To be honest, I do not feel that I deserve to be in the company of so many of the transformative figures who have been honored by this prize, men and women who've inspired me and inspired the entire world through their courageous pursuit of peace."

He became the third sitting president to ever receive the prestigious award, allowing him to join the company of Mikhail Gorbachev, Nelson Mandela, and many others making history. Obama donated the $1.4 million prize to several charities.

Barack Obama began the first part of his presidency in a flurry of excitement. As the months stretched into years, this president achieved several of his goals, including a valiant attempt at healthcare reform and settling the score with Osama bin Laden.

Four years later at the second Obama inauguration, as I stood on the north media riser (not a great vantage point), I looked over with fond memories across the crowd at my former spectacular location. My position had a view of the back of the president for the swearing in, and disappointed as I was, there was nothing I could do about it.

Above: Obama's posse;
Top right: An emotional president;
Bottom right: Negotiating peacemakers Abbas of Palestine and Netanyahu of Israel.

Panning across the VIP section, I realized I had a great view of all the Supreme Court justices, a photographic opportunity I had sought for years. Following the swearing in, President Obama turned to kiss the first lady as his daughters looked on, and I found I was in just the right spot for that uncommon picture.

Shortly after the inauguration, we members of the Press Corps eagerly waited to see what changes this new

The first lady harvests her garden with local school kids.

administration would bring. Sadly, access became more limited as two waves in the Oval Office were reduced to one by order of the president himself and a policy of responding to events via RSVP became the new normal.

Aside from the everyday work issues, I saw some touching situations during the Obama administration, like witnessing Vice President Biden in an unusually close moment with Speaker of the House John Boehner. Another special memory was watching as Presidents Obama and Clinton enjoyed a playful encounter during a ceremony in the East Room.

In contrast, there were also emotional times for all of us at the Obama White House. The day President Obama gave a speech on gun control, he invited the family members of shooting victims, including some of the parents of the children killed in the Sandy Hook massacre. Even the media was emotional at that powerful event as we shed tears along with the president.

President Obama also gathered Middle East leaders to foster peaceful relationships. He hosted a summit attended by President Mahmoud Abbas of Palestine and Prime Minister Benjamin Netanyahu of Israel. I was fortunate to have a front row seat to witness those two conflicted leaders share a gentle moment.

First lady Michelle Obama initiated a wonderful program called "Let's Move," educating children on healthy eating and exercise. She even started a garden at the White House, as she invited grade-school children to participate in both planting and harvesting vegetables and then showed the kids how to prepare dishes with that same food. Michelle Obama also targeted the high school student population as she brought icons in the fields of fashion, music and poetry to the White House to talk with aspiring designers, musicians and writers.

President Obama honored many talented people from all walks of life, including

Michelle Obama shares tender moments with her family and dog; President Obama walks with his daughters Malia and Sasha.

Chapter 20 | President Barack Obama

President Obama high-fives kids at an Easter Egg Roll.

Presidents H.W. Bush and Bill Clinton, who were each awarded the Presidential Medal of Freedom. Presidential friendships seemed to be forged as the previous commander in chiefs truly appreciated what the present leader had to bear.

The Obama family seemed genuinely a tight-knit unit, dogs and all. It was interesting to see how after all those years in office, the family still had some natural moments in front of both the Secret Service protective detail and the crowds of people surrounding them. I was thankful to witness elder daughter, Malia, having a tender moment with her mom at the 2014 Easter Egg Roll, while at the same time, her dad was greeting his young and exuberant constituents.

However, most presidential occurrences belong to the public and to history. In a democracy, it is the role of the press to document an objective, truthful record. ✦

Chapter 21

Lest Ye Be Judged

Supreme Court justices, appointed for life, spend their careers applying their legal expertise, their personal standards of right and wrong, and their individual political interpretations of the constitution to landmark cases. Before being trusted with such history making roles, they themselves are vetted by Congress. Like other defendants, they find their words and actions often removed from all relevant context, exposed, scrutinized, and evaluated in public. During the confirmation hearings, a youthful indiscretion, an off-the-cuff remark, or an outdated judicial rendering may become tomorrow's headlines. Their own "day on trial" can be a trying one indeed.

— Professor Ruth Egan Dalton

Chief Justice John Roberts
Confirmation Hearings
Hart Bldg., Room 216
Capitol Hill
Sept. 12, 2005

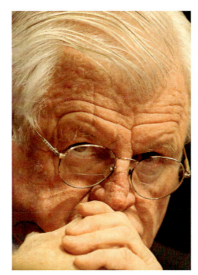

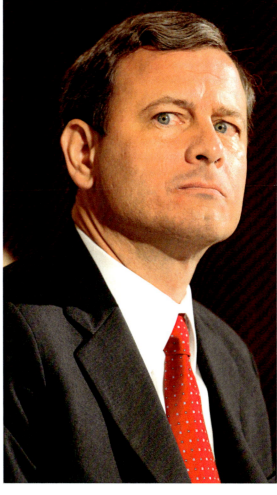

Chief Justice Roberts
Confirmation Hearings
Hart Building,
Room 216
Capitol Hill
Sept. 12-14, 2005

I COVERED MANY different types of confirmation hearings over the years, but this one really impressed me: Wow! History was happening right there! Right then! That hearing was my first experience photographing a prospective member of the Supreme Court going through the confirmation process. The drama was intensified because that was in fact the big cheese: the chief justice of the United States.

Senator Arlen Specter, who was the chairman of the Judiciary Committee and an ally of the Washington Press Corps, led the proceedings with his gracious style, while Senator Ted Kennedy presided in his own fashion. As is tradition, after the chairman made his opening statement, the Democrats and Republicans who sat

EYES THAT SPEAK **127**

Chapter 21 | Lest Ye Be Judged

John Roberts is sworn in as chief justice of the Supreme Court by Justice John Paul Stevens.

on either side of him took turns asking questions of the witness. John Roberts, in my opinion, did a phenomenal job appropriately responding, deflecting and avoiding the questions fired at him, many regarding his position on abortion and capital punishment.

The most memorable part of the proceedings to me were the remarks by Senator Lindsey Graham of South Carolina stating he was aware of the responsibility that he and the other senators on the Judiciary Committee shared, because this particular decision would affect the lives of generations to come, should Roberts be confirmed. I was sitting directly beneath him in the "photographers' well" and could hear everything that was said. With great emotion, he wished the angels to be with Roberts and the senators in their decision. To me it was a very powerful, moving portion of the proceedings.

The range of emotions that each witness seemed to experience over the days of testimony during the confirmation process was like a roller-coaster ride.

Chief Justice John Roberts'
Swearing-in Ceremony
The East Room of the White House
Sept. 29, 2005

EVENTUALLY, AND WITH minimal notice, we were informed that the swearing in of Chief Justice Roberts would be taking place in the East Room of the White House. I suspected one reason for the short notice was to avoid huge crowds. Luckily, I made it just in time and was able to get a great position. Even the most seasoned photographers seemed to have some anxiety about recording that moment in history. We double-checked our settings, cleaned our lenses a couple of extra times and awaited the beginning of the ceremony. After what seemed like a very long time, President Bush made his remarks, followed by Supreme Court Justice John Paul Stevens administering the oath of office to Roberts, the new Chief Justice, as his wife, Jane, held the Bible.

Justice Samuel Alito
Confirmation Hearings
Hart Bldg., Room 216
Capitol Hill
Jan. 9, 2006

Candidate Samuel Alito and his supporters: his wife, Martha (in red), and Eunice Kennedy Shriver (below right).

THE NEXT CONFIRMATION hearing I covered was Justice Samuel Alito. What I remember most about this proceeding was the candidate being grilled about his affiliation with the now-defunct club "the Concerned Alumni of Princeton." The conservative group of students on the Princeton campus were involved in various causes, including limiting the number of women admitted to the university and those who were allowed to join the clubs on campus.

During the confirmation hearings, Alito distanced himself from that group, whose views had been seen as both sexist and racist. He testified, "I disavow them. I deplore them. They represent things that I have always stood against, and I can't express too strongly." Alito's wife, Martha, burst into tears after Republicans showed their disapproval of how Alito was being portrayed by some Democrats on the panel. Sadly enough, I was in the ladies' room when that took place. Timing is everything.

However, as I had previously learned, each person nominated for a position on the U.S. Supreme Court bench had to really put his or her entire life before the Senate and the rest of the world to examine. With each confirmation hearing, there always seemed to be a particular issue or comment that was highlighted and analyzed by the members of the committee.

The verbal volley that happened between various witnesses and the senators engaged not only the players but also their family members, as they watched

Chapter 21 | Lest Ye Be Judged

Justice-to-be Sonia Sotomayor volleys with Senator Patrick Leahy (right) as her emotional family looks on.

their loved ones being dissected under the microscope of scrutiny.

Each hearing took on a life and personality of its own, while it was basically the same process with a different cast of characters. Every now and then we spotted a famous face in the audience such as Eunice Kennedy Schriver intensely watching the proceedings.

Justice Sonia Sotomayor
Confirmation Hearing
Hart Bldg., Room 216
July 13, 2009

IRONICALLY, IT WAS while still covering those hearings about the highest level of justice in the country that my personal style of connecting with my subjects collided with the guidelines of the House and Senate. I made the mistake of becoming more at ease with the familiarity of the drill. I unwittingly violated an unwritten law by speaking to a witness: Sonia Sotomayor.

I was positioned in "the well" — the space in between the witness and the Senate committee. The photographers were allowed to stand there until the gavel was struck by the committee chairman. At that point, we had to stay crouched down because the TV cameras were rolling, and we needed to ensure that we

130   EYES THAT SPEAK

were not blocking the view. In that case, the chairman was Senator Patrick Leahy, a wonderful friend to the photographers, as he was a bit of a photographer himself.

On the first day of her hearings, Judge Sotomayor exited the chambers and was heading into the hearing room. As she made her way to the witness table, she was greeted by her family and friends in the front row. Sotomayor continued to hobble down onto the hearing room floor, her leg in a cast from a fractured ankle. One side of the crowd was transformed into a human aisle where friends were cheering her on in an enthusiastic but subdued manner. They patted her on the shoulder, shook her hand or gave her a hug and mentioned their support as she worked her way toward the witness table, where she was about to testify. It felt like a receiving line of sorts. Suddenly, Sotomayor turned to me and our eyes locked. I wanted to wish her luck and so I said, "Break a leg out there."

She smiled and replied, "I've already done that!"

Later, I was reprimanded, but was allowed to continue photographing throughout the three-day hearing. The big "issue" in her case was that when she was giving a speech to law students at a graduation ceremony, she had stated, "I would hope that a wise, Latina woman with the richness of her experiences would more often than not reach a better conclusion than a white male who hasn't lived that life."

That statement really rocked the block on Capitol Hill. Senator after senator questioned her relentlessly. She continued to hold her ground, saying that she was attempting to encourage those who had a difficult background and — I believe — to give the message that from our past experiences, as Friedrich Nietzsche was quoted as saying, "What doesn't kill you makes you stronger and often wiser."

Aspiring Justice Elena Kagan reacts to questions from the Judiciary Committee.

As her family witnessed the hearing from the front row, strong emotions emerged. It seemed to me that was her "hot coals" subject, which she needed to address in order for the Senate Judiciary Committee to believe in her and give their stamp of approval. In my opinion, she danced across those coals.

Justice Elena Kagan
Confirmation Hearings
Hart Bldg. Room 216
June 28, 2010

AND THEN CAME Elena Kagan a year later. Her controversial issue? She had kicked the military recruiters off the Harvard campus when she was acting dean of students before becoming the 11th dean of Harvard Law School. I noted that a common response used by all the different nominees was that they wanted to avoid publicly prejudging a legal subject or case that may come before them one day. That gave them a wonderful excuse not to answer some of the questions that were too defining of their individual, personal character.

She said, "I think that if there are positions that you can't argue, then the responsibility is probably to resign. If one's own conscience is opposed to the requirements and responsibilities of the job, then it's time to leave the job."

She, too, successfully avoided expressing personal views on issues such as abortion and gun control, yet she seemed to enjoy sparring with her questioners. For some of the questions, there was no right answer and there was certainly more humor at the Kagan hearing than any of the others I had covered.

After all the opening remarks, it came time for her to swear in and begin her testimony. Regretfully, I had been assigned a position much farther away from the witness than usual but made the best of it. (Later, I learned that I was being penalized for speaking to the previous witness, Sotomayor, a year earlier.) I took the

Chapter 21 | Lest Ye Be Judged

They emerged from their confirmation hearings, transformed, finally, from witness to judge.

For Elena Kagan, each day of hearings brought new challenges.

customary pictures from my remote position with a restless feeling of frustration at being away from the front lines.

As Elena Kagan left the hearing room during a break, she walked under my position in "the slit," an opening in a balcony above her. Without thinking, as she walked by, I wished her good luck. She looked up, smiled and said "Thanks." I got myself in deep trouble with those two words because I was talking with the witness. Again. I gave up the opportunity for a shot knowing that the next day would be the payoff, because I had established a connection with my subject no matter how small it was. After being placed in what I called a "time out," I was not allowed on the Senate floor and back in the well again until later that day.

Even though my pride was wounded, I needed to accept the rules of the road and go against my instincts of communicating with my subjects, which for me always led to a better and more intimate picture. Although hard for me, I totally understood. If each of us talked to the various witnesses, things would become chaotic.

It pained me as I looked down from my same spot the next day and noticed Judge Kagan looking up at my position as I quietly took a picture. Before having offered encouragement, my voice was now silenced. I could not speak any friendly words of support for fear of getting into even more trouble. Nevertheless, it was not worth losing the trust of those with whom I worked. Every now and then we all needed to look up from our cameras and see the bigger picture.

Aspiring Justice Neil Gorsuch addresses the Judiciary Committee.
Right: Justice Gorsuch is sworn in by his mentor Justice Anthony Kennedy.

Justice Neil Gorsuch
Confirmation Hearings
Hart Bldg., Room 216
March 22, 2017

PRESIDENT TRUMP'S first nomination, Neil Gorsuch, faced the Judiciary Committee in an effort to fill the spot of the late Justice Antonin Scalia. Big shoes to fill. Gorsuch very calmly refused to answer questions from Democrats about abortion, gun control and a few other topics, citing that those subjects could come up before the U.S. Supreme Court in the future.

Gorsuch remarked, "I have offered no promises on how I'd rule in any case to anyone, and I don't think it's appropriate for a judge to do so," pledging to keep an open mind.

This judicial candidate used different words, but the same argument as Justice Kagan had used in her confirmation hearing.

He did say that "no man is above the law" when asked if he would ever rule against President Trump if necessary. Throughout it all, he seemed quite calm and composed.

On April 10, 2017, in the Rose Garden, Judge Gorsuch took the oath of office. As his former boss, Supreme Court Justice Anthony Kennedy, read the oath, his wife, Louise, held the Bible, and he looked up smiling at his children sitting in the front row, witnessing history.

Chapter 21 | Lest Ye Be Judged

Justice Brett Kavanaugh
Confirmation Hearings
Hart Bldg., Room 216
Sept. 3-4, 2018

THE NEWS OF Justice Anthony Kennedy's resignation swept through the White House, and less than two weeks later, President Trump nominated Brett Kavanaugh. He had clerked for Kennedy in the past and would be taking his seat if confirmed.

After looking through my archives, I found the image of a younger Kavanaugh as he was being sworn in by Justice Kennedy for the position of judge for the District Court of Appeals in 2006. I am sure he never dreamed he would come full circle and be nominated for his mentor's seat as justice of the U.S. Supreme Court.

That hearing was by far the most contentious of all that I had covered. Democrats united in an attempt to postpone the hearing due to insufficient documents, while more than 60 protesters inside the hearing room challenged that nominee's record and his influence on the future. All of that on day one. Following that three-day hearing, just as the committee was about to vote, Dr. Christine Blasey Ford came forward alleging a drunken Kavanaugh had sexually assaulted her when they were teenagers at a party.

Kavanaugh had responded in his remarks defending himself: "This whole two-week effort has been a calculated and orchestrated political hit, fueled with apparent pent-up anger about President Trump and the 2016 election, fear that has been unfairly stoked about my judicial record, revenge on behalf of the Clintons and millions of dollars in money from outside left-wing opposition groups. This is a circus ... This grotesque and coordinated character assassination will dissuade confident and good people of all political persuasions from serving our country."

The #MeToo movement exploded across the country, more allegations came forward and an FBI investigation was ordered. Both the Kavanaugh family and the Ford family went through intense media scrutiny as the country awaited the results of the investigation. One week later, the Senate approved Brett

Nominee Kavanaugh gets emotional during the questioning.

Kavanaugh answers questions during his confirmation hearings.

During Kavanaugh's interview, protesters continually interrupted the process.

EYES THAT SPEAK 135

Chapter 21 | Lest Ye Be Judged

Left: Protesters watch the testimony of Christine Blasey Ford; signage covers the White House perimeter.

Kavanaugh to be the next U.S. justice of the Supreme Court.

During the swearing-in ceremony at the White House, President Trump began his remarks with "On behalf of our nation, I want to apologize to Brett and the entire Kavanaugh family for the terrible pain and suffering you have been forced to endure."

Justice Kavanaugh responded, "The Senate confirmation process was contentious and emotional. That process is over. My focus now is to be the best justice I can be. I take this office with gratitude and no bitterness." He looked over at his supportive friends and former classmates in the audience and with emotion, told them he loved them.

On Oct. 8, 2018, after weeks of controversy, Kavanaugh is sworn in by Justice Stevens as President Trump and Kavanaugh's family look on.

Protestors and supporters gather outside the Supreme Court as Judge Amy Coney Barrett prepared to meet with members of the Senate.

Justice Amy Coney Barrett
Confirmation Hearings
Hart Bldg., Room 216
Oct. 13, 2020

JUDGE AMY CONEY BARRETT'S confirmation hearing to replace Justice Ruth Bader Ginsburg began less than two weeks after Ginsburg was laid to rest in Arlington cemetery, igniting a series of protests.

The Barrett hearing became controversial when Democrats wanted the next Supreme Court Justice to be chosen by the next U.S. president since Trump had already nominated Kavanaugh and Gorsuch, who were conservatives.

Judge Amy Coney Barrett's hearing was held during the COVID-19 pandemic, restricting most of us media from being allowed in the room because of social distancing guidelines. I was thankful to be able to go into that hearing, although only for a brief time was able to catch a few nice moments.

Barrett seemed very knowledgeable and gave everyone a smile during her interaction with Senator Cornyn.

"You know most of us have multiple notebooks, and notes, and books and things like that in front of us," Cornyn said. "Can you hold up what you've been referring to in answering our questions? Is there anything on it?" Cornyn asked.

Barrett cracked a smile and held up a blank notepad that was sitting in front of her.

Chapter 21 | Lest Ye Be Judged

The big two issues at this hearing were about her stance on gun control and pro-life. Judge Barrett revealed that she and her family did own a gun, and she seemed confident she would continue to be a good working mom to her large family should she be confirmed.

LOOKING BACK ON the Supreme Court justices I had covered, I reflected on the "big picture" which spans the many years of those justices deciding cases that would affect both people's lives and the country's future. I wondered how many of them would empathize with the stressed defendants sitting before them once they emerged from their confirmation hearings, transformed, finally, from witness to judge. ✪

Judge Amy Coney Barrett testifying before the Senate.

On Oct. 27, 2020, Justice Amy Coney Barrett was sworn in to fill the seat left vacant by Ruth Bader Ginsburg. Crowds — both for and against — once again filled the streets of Washington, D.C.

138 EYES THAT SPEAK

Chapter 22

Dustup at the China State Arrival

THE MEETING REQUIRED more than a year of intensive diplomacy to arrange and was postponed by Hurricane Katrina. It emphasized the long list of tensions between one of the world's richest countries and its fastest-rising competitor.

All seemed normal as the official state visit began and I secured my position on the press platform. I looked around to see if I might have a better vantage point if I moved down the three-tiered riser to the next level. Before doing so, I noticed a member of the visiting Chinese press appraising where I was standing. I offered her my position as I stepped down to a lower level on the riser.

Things got off to a rocky start as the announcer mistakenly confused the official name of China with that of Taiwan, which China claims as part of its sovereign territory. Then President Bush made his welcoming remarks, turning the podium over to President Hu Jintao.

Suddenly, the journalist who inherited my spot on the top riser began yelling at the top of her voice at the Chinese head of state. She cried out, "President Bush, stop him from persecuting the Falun Gong! President Hu, your days are numbered!" I wonder how many sharpshooters positioned on the roof of the White House simultaneously set their sights on her. Because she was above me, her spit rained down on several of us as she continued to scream. What started out as a mediocre spot turned into "the place to be," as lenses and guns pointed in our direction.

President Hu Jintao of China
White House State Arrival Ceremony
April 20, 2006

President Bush with President Hu Jintao of China

A protester briefly interrupts the ceremony.

Chapter 22 | Dustup at the China State Arrival

President Bush reviews the troops with President Hu. Right: Protesters yell outside the White House.

I wonder how many sharpshooters positioned on the roof of the White House simultaneously set their sights on her.

President Bush turned to his staff with a look that I interpreted to mean shut this person up and get back to the ceremony.

Meanwhile, out in front of the White House on Pennsylvania Avenue, bullhorns amplified chanting messages from hundreds of protesters which disrupted the ceremony. President Hu looked worried that perhaps the protesters had infiltrated the White House. He was right. The now 47-year-old Dr. Wang Wenyi, a Chinese-born U.S. resident and member of the suppressed Falun Gong spiritual movement, had gotten inside with media credentials and tried to boldly dominate the ceremony. That woman had several minutes of airtime. The Secret Service agents positioned closest to us could not easily get to her on the crowded risers because they had to climb over many tripods holding the television cameras and still photographers.

After agents finally dragged her away, the program resumed, with only a hiccup to protocol. Security heightened noticeably. Several of us shook our heads and worried about that foreign reporter's fate after she was quickly escorted from public view. That of course was a major embarrassment for both presidents. I later learned that all Chinese television networks went to black during that incident.

Much to my surprise, the next week, after being released from jail, Dr. Wenyi, the screaming protester, was invited by the Newsmaker Committee to speak at the National Press Club. Only in America.

On Sept. 25, 2015, President Xi Jinping and his wife, Madame Peng Liyuan, were invited by the Obamas to the White House for an official state visit. There were fewer risers that time and you could be sure there was a clear pathway to the media area as a routine state visit unfolded with no complications. ✪

Sept. 25, 2015

TEN YEARS LATER, the White House hosted China again for an official state arrival ceremony under the Obama administration.

This time, President Jinping Xi arrived under tranquil circumstances, only 48 hours after Pope Francis had trod the same special space. Congeniality reigned.

140   EYES THAT SPEAK

Chapter 23

The Rich, Famous and Just Plain Cool

DURING THE COURSE OF MY CAREER, I have been fortunate enough to have had the opportunity to photograph some outstanding, treasured icons from all walks of life. Whether they be from Hollywood, Dollywood, the boxing ring or the Rock and Roll Hall of Fame, these folks made a special impression on me and made their mark on the world.

Barbra Streisand
The multi-talented, award-winning singer, songwriter, actress and filmmaker has a career spanning six decades adding the 2015 Presidential Medal of Freedom to her list of achievements. During the ceremony, Streisand looked out at her family and friends in the audience as she waited with anticipation to hear President Obama call her name and present her with her latest honor.

Muhammad Ali
I was impressed with Ali's positive attitude when I photographed this legendary boxer several times prior to the decline of his health due to Parkinson's disease. The fighter's spirit remained strong as he joked with me while he performed puppet tricks and feigned beating me up. I noticed that Ali seemed to enjoy entertaining various members of the press each time I photographed him. He used to say, "I am so mean, I make medicine sick!" When Ali passed away, thousands of his fans turned out to pay their respects from all over the country.

Cal Ripken Jr.
"The Iron Man," the Hall of Fame infielder for the Baltimore Orioles, was certainly the nice guy that I always heard about. This baseball legend with blazing blue eyes kindly gave each fan in the room his undivided attention during a private reception. When asked about his success and fame, he humbly replied, "To be remembered at all is pretty cool." Ripken has started youth camps and coaching clinics, dedicated to teaching kids the game as he "pays it forward" to the future children of baseball.

EYES THAT SPEAK   141

Chapter 23 | The Rich, Famous and Just Plain Cool

Dolly Parton

I was surprised to learn that Dolly Parton is an amazing businesswoman. She comes across as very genuine, cracking jokes with self-deprecating humor, yet she is bursting with confidence. Dolly's simple but elegant quote, "If you want a rainbow, you need to put up with a little rain," is characteristic of her.

I was also impressed with the force by which she continues to give back to the Appalachian community where she grew up as a very poor child. Each month, this award-winning singer donates a new, carefully selected book via Dolly Parton's Imagination Library to all five-year-old children of Cumberland County, North Carolina, to familiarize them with reading skills and prepare them for school. In addition, Dolly has opened an amusement park, "Dollywood," providing jobs for many in her area.

Oprah Winfrey

Winfrey is a woman of many talents: journalist, philanthropist, publisher, actress, producer and talk show host, and even owns her own television network, OWN. In 2003, Winfrey became the first African American woman to become a billionaire in the United States. She was awarded the Presidential Medal of Freedom in 2013.

I believe she deserves a special shout-out for founding the Oprah Winfrey Leadership Academy for Girls in South Africa. It is there that she continues to "provide a nurturing educational environment for academically gifted girls who come from disadvantaged backgrounds."

Meryl Streep

This brilliant, award-winning actress has fascinated audiences everywhere with her ability to take on versatile, powerful roles on screen. I was surprised by her shy demeanor as she accepted the 2014 Presidential Medal of Freedom from President Obama. While introducing the actress, the president joked, "I am in love with Meryl. Both Michelle and Meryl's husband know it, but there is nothing I can do about it." Streep gave him a shy smile and blushed.

Ellen DeGeneres

This courageous entertainer, who in her own life knows the meaning of redemption, once traded her career for her beliefs.

She paid a heavy price as she came out about her sexuality. Her kind and relatable humor has helped her triumph over adversity and led to hosting an award-winning talk show for many years. On the day she arrived at the White House with her mom and wife, Portia, DeGeneres had forgotten her drivers' license and was temporarily denied admission inside. Once things were sorted out, Ellen found herself on stage in the East Room of the White House, where President Obama praised her benevolent style of humor as he presented her with the Presidential Medal of Freedom.

Robert De Niro

America's famous "gangster actor" is also known to impersonate taxi drivers and has played in a variety of psychological thrillers. I was touched by his show of compassion to Ellen DeGeneres during her overwhelming moment at the Presidential Medal of Freedom ceremony in 2016. Medal recipients were seated in alphabetical order on the stage when this tender moment unfolded as DeGeneres was overcome with emotion and was comforted by De Niro. This scene embodies why I wrote this book. Reacting on a personal level, a renowned actor saw an opportunity to be human and speak with a hug. Having the opportunity to witness genuine moments like that, from time to time, stand out as I record human nature revealing itself in front of my camera.

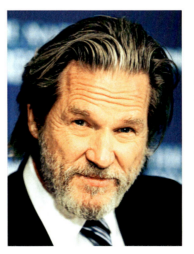

Jeff Bridges

This actor had taken on the mission of trying to help end childhood hunger in the United States. He founded the End Hunger Network and employs a state-to-state method of targeting the problem. He was an engaging subject to everyone he encountered, including myself.

Aretha Franklin

Aretha Franklin, another award-winning singer, songwriter and pianist, started out as a gospel singer in her dad's Baptist church and went on to become the Queen of Soul. Franklin's many accomplishments include singing at President Obama's first inauguration and receiving the Presidential Medal of Freedom from President George W. Bush. Franklin's famous rendition of "Respect" has earned her a timeless place in music.

Bruce Springsteen

Known as "The Boss," the award-winning singer and songwriter has entertained generations of fans with his music about everyday American life. Growing up near the Jersey shore, Springsteen succeeded in tapping into the small-town, American culture and crafting songs about people who often have felt forgotten. During his normally sold-out performances, he is famous for bringing his audience to their feet, for three hours plus, dancing to his music. I was fortunate enough to experience Springsteen on Broadway, and although cameras were not permitted, I did come away with a treasured handshake.

Danica Patrick

Aside from taking on a career in the male-dominated world of NASCAR and Indy racing, Danica Patrick emits a calm and composed demeanor. She is feminine yet has a strong presence. Three days after I photographed her, she seriously crashed at the Daytona 500.

This petite woman impressed her fellow drivers as she expertly maneuvered her car during the high-speed crash. As the accident unfolded, Patrick remained cool as she applied all the appropriate techniques to survive the accident. She escaped from the crushed vehicle, unharmed and probably wiser.

"The Times They Are A-Changin'"

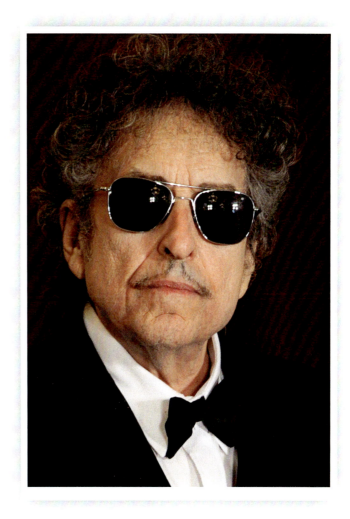

DYLAN'S MUSIC HAS always been a part of my life and has inspired a generation. Almost everyone has heard his songs, whether sung by him or someone else. After I learned that he was to be one of the honorees of the year for the prestigious Presidential Medal of Freedom award, I was excited that I would have a chance to photograph the legendary Bob Dylan.

Racing across town that morning, I unfortunately missed the preset opportunity for the East Room and a friend kindly saved me a spot in the head-on position. Rumor had it that Dylan would be sitting on the far left of the stage, so photographers positioned ourselves accordingly. I made a quick trip to the restroom, and within those five minutes everything had changed. Bob Dylan had been relocated to the far right as White House staffers realized his birth name was Robert Zimmerman and placed him at the end of the alphabetical lineup. Almost all the photographers had stormed to the opposite side of the room for a better view of the renowned musician. With 30 minutes or so before the event, I looked around to assess the situation.

I quickly noticed that the stepladder securing my place had been moved about four feet during my absence. I asked a photographer whom I had never seen before what happened. He smugly told me he thought I had left so he took my spot. Then he refused to relinquish it. I asked a White House staffer about this and was told, "You guys handle it between yourselves." There was nothing I could do about it.

Fortunately, a fellow photographer saw the dustup from across the room and graciously yelled for me to come over to get the spot that I had "requested" she save for me. Grateful for her little white lie, I picked up my gear and, leaving my stepladder behind, triumphantly made my way over to the preferable section of the media-packed room. Once there, I found a small, abandoned ladder, which the previous photographer probably was not able to take when everyone quickly changed positions. As I scoped out my newfound place, using this small metal ladder with narrow steps, I discovered that I needed to lean out even farther to shoot past the long lenses of my fellow photographers, who were already pressed up against the red velvet ropes separating the media from the guests.

After standing on the narrow rungs of the metal ladder for a while, a shooting pain began to radiate through my feet, up my legs and into my spine. I bent down to the guest, his chair pressed up against the rope line next to me and asked if he would mind if I leaned in a couple inches closer to him, which would have made a big difference for my shot. He replied that I could, but only if I gave him a copy of all the pictures I was about to take for that event. I declined and politely gave him a suggestion.

I think most of the pictures taken by the photographers in the room that day could not help but portray Bob Dylan's smokin' cool demeanor. Some of us just had to work harder than others to get the image.

Bob Dylan
The White House Presidential Medal of Freedom Awards
May 25, 2012

Chapter 23 | The Rich, Famous and Just Plain Cool

George Clooney
This handsome actor dominated the interest of men and women alike at the National Press Club. Although I seemed to notice more of the ladies taking a deep breath as they admired his sexy presence. Clooney, along with his father, continues to be passionate about using his voice to heighten awareness and improve the terrible conditions in Darfur.

Angelina Jolie
I had photographed her during her tenure as the appointed Goodwill Ambassador for the United Nations High Commissioner for Refugees in Geneva, Switzerland. Ms. Jolie was surprisingly critical of the many camera flashes that captured her every move. She went on to speak of the charitable causes that she endorses. I especially admire her efforts in bringing awareness to the strife concerning women's rights regarding breast cancer in Bosnia and her personal struggle with the same issue. Attentive to childhood adoption issues, she and ex-husband Brad Pitt adopted kids from other countries in addition to their biological children.

Venus Williams
In 2002, Venus Williams was the first African American woman to achieve number one ranking in tennis in the Open Era. She has won an Olympic Gold Medal in four separate games. Both she and her younger sister, Serena — her doubles partner — are an unbeatable grand slam duo.

Venus spoke at the National Press Club of the lessons she has learned from her failures and how they have propelled her. Williams noted that she and her younger sister, Serena, rarely talked about tennis but when they did, they rehashed their mistakes and not the great shots they made. She emphasized that discipline is crucial. Venus revealed the following: "We were always setting goals. We were always taught to set goals and write them down. My dad said, 'Don't have it in your head, always have it on paper.' And I find that becomes something very important. When you see it with your eyes, it somehow goes into your head and becomes visual, and becomes something real."

Mariska Hargitay

Hargitay has an unusual story. I appreciated that she did not ride on the fame of her mother, actress Jayne Mansfield, who tragically died in a car accident when Mariska was a young child. As a successful actress herself, in the popular series "Law and Order SVU" (Special Victims Unit), Hargitay began to receive letters requesting autographed pictures. She also noticed a growing number of fans who were writing her and confessing their real-life sexual abuse secrets to her character on the show, Detective Olivia Benson. Many had never revealed those experiences until a particular episode on the show affected them personally. The writers of the show have even used some of the letters sent to the actress as inspiration for story lines.

As a result, Hargitay launched the Joyful Heart Foundation to help the real-life victims of sexual abuse. I find it admirable that she has taken the serious role that she plays on TV and parlayed it into helping survivors of domestic violence, child abuse and sexual assault by giving them a voice off-screen.

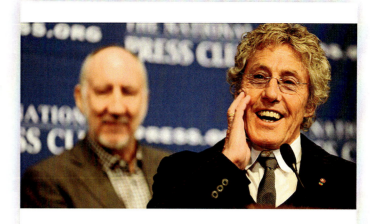

The Who

Having grown up with their music, I have always been a fan and was thrilled to score this assignment at the National Press Club. Lead singer, Roger Daltrey, and lead guitarist, Pete Townshend, longtime friends, are the last surviving members of the original lineup. They set aside time from performing to help promote Teen Cancer America. The foundation, created in 2011, by Daltrey and Townshend, is based at Ronald Reagan UCLA Medical Center. The pair plans to expand Teen Cancer America. This program sets up units in hospitals and medical centers in special areas around the United States. They both have supported a comparable program in Great Britain known as the Teenage Cancer Trust. Once again, I found it inspiring to see legendary performers use their fame to help others in need.

Mick Jagger

Lead singer, songwriter and co-founder of the legendary band, the Rolling Stones, Jagger has been in the spotlight performing for over six decades. Although I was only permitted to photograph the Rolling Stones for three songs, it was very cool to be up close and personal as they danced across the stage playing their classic songs, their sweat occasionally spattering on us photographers. We had to really hustle to keep up with their movements and make the most of our time with them while still appreciating their talents.

Robert Redford

The world knows him as a sexy heartthrob, award-winning actor, director, producer, environmentalist and founder of the Sundance Film Festival. Upon meeting this movie star legend — "Butch Cassidy and the Sundance Kid" is one of my favorites — Redford was at the White House to receive the Presidential Medal of Freedom and he was kind enough to come visit the media following the award ceremony. I was amazed at how humble this man was as I shook his hand, and he shared that at 80 years of age, he wished that his mom and dad had been at the White House ceremony to see him receive this highly respected honor from the president of the United States.

"So often in life, things that you regard as an impediment turn out to be great, good fortune."

The Notorious RBG

JUSTICE RUTH BADER GINSBURG, the second woman ever confirmed to the U.S. Supreme Court, had over the years become a pop culture icon and a warrior for gender equality. Known for her brilliant career in law, she was a tireless advocate for women's rights and was quoted, "So often in life, things that you regard as an impediment turn out to be great, good fortune."

I had the honor of photographing Justice Ginsburg in 2016. She was petite but had a very big presence. People around her seemed to be intimidated as she went about just being herself.

If possible, I always attempt to make a connection with my subjects — especially when I am the only photographer — creating a bridge that bypasses the big camera that is between us.

My next-door neighbor was the former Deputy Solicitor General at the Supreme Court and I thought that would be an easy icebreaker with Justice Ginsburg. Not so. When I asked if she knew him, she snapped, "Of course I do." I quickly switched gears and offered my condolences to her for the loss of her friend three months earlier — Justice Antonin Scalia. The tension broke immediately, and she went on to reply, "Thank you. He will be greatly missed. There will never be another like him."

She spoke about them going to dinners and operas together, and the upcoming film that was coming out on her life story.

Four years later, I was covering the public gathered at the Supreme Court to pay tribute to Justice Ginsburg the day after she had passed away at the age of 87. Flowers, candles, photographs and notes were placed outside the court as people stood in silence with the occasional sounds of weeping.

Hundreds of mourners came to pay their respects to Ginsburg at the Supreme Court as she laid in repose outside the front door of the building, making a very dramatic statement about her career there. During a private ceremony, Chief Justice Roberts said, "Ruth wanted to be an opera virtuoso but became a rock star instead."

During the private ceremony, he spoke about her battles against gender discrimination throughout her career.

Finally, her remains were brought over to the U.S. Capitol, led by a woman Marine, where she laid in state for a couple of hours for the members of Congress to pay their final respects. As RBG was brought out of the Capitol, the stairs were lined with female members of Congress, each of whom had been impacted by the tiny powerhouse of a woman, the Notorious RBG.

Justice Ginsburg's body is brought to the Capitol. The first female to lay in state there in U.S. history.

Chapter 23 | The Rich, Famous and Just Plain Cool

FOR YEARS EACH DAY, I exited the metro station and crossed over to Farragut Square Park on my way to the White House. I would always get a cheerful "Hi there!" from a man seated on a bench surrounded by bags piled high with personal belongings. Eventually, I slowly began an extraordinary friendship with this amazing homeless man named Homer. He was the definition of cool. Homer had become a park fixture, just like the various sculptures around the Washington, D.C., area that many of us took for granted.

For years, like the other commuters, I had barely paid much attention to him as I briskly walked by in an effort to get to my job on time. I learned after getting to know him that he had been sitting in the park for many years, moving from one side to the other as a survival technique — shade versus sun depending on the season. He chose that park because of his admiration for General Farragut and his leadership of the troops he had commanded.

One hot spring morning, I was coming from photographing a physically demanding job prior to going to cover the White House, and I felt a bit faint. I paused to say hello to Homer as usual. Homer noticed I was not feeling well and asked me to sit down with him and suggested that maybe I needed something to eat. Homer pointed to the many bags surrounding him. "Take whatever you need. You are welcome to anything of mine that you want," he generously motioned, sweeping his arms toward his bags. He boasted of the generous people who looked out for him on their way to work, leaving him food donations. I chose a package of peanut butter crackers and a bottle of water. Before long, I began to feel my strength return.

A week or so later, I happened to be transporting several cumbersome prints to the National Press Club (located near the White House) for the annual Members' Photography Exhibit. The White House was my first stop of the day. Noticing I was hauling more than my usual equipment, Homer asked what I was up to. He then asked to see my exhibit images. I showed him my prints of Queen Elizabeth II I had taken earlier in the year from her

Homer
A Friend of
Farragut Square Park
and a Friend of Mine

arrival ceremony at the White House. Homer pleaded to come to the exhibit and assured me that he would clean up nice, and that he had "dress up clothes" in a storage locker that contained several of his "good" belongings. In addition, he assured me he would act appropriately.

With his outgoing manner, I had no doubt he could hold his own anywhere. I was more concerned that someone would embarrass him if he were recognized.

I gave him the address of the event and the time of the opening reception. I was chatting with other friends at the reception and as the crowd began to swell, I noticed Homer enter from across the room. He looked great and as I gave him a big hug, I noticed he smelled good too. I proudly began introducing him to my friends and other members of the Press Club. Homer made creative small talk as he shook hands and chatted with the president of the National Press Club.

One of my photographer buddies did recognize him and was surprised by his transformation, whispering to me, "Isn't that the homeless guy from the bench at Farragut Park?"

As everyone began to mingle, I asked Homer if he would like anything to drink, thinking I would flag down one of the waiters. Homer said that he wanted a Budweiser, which was not one of the drinks offered, and so off he went to find one. I did not see him for at least an hour. When he suddenly appeared, he was sporting his big, toothless grin. He had been careful to smile with his mouth closed when he had first arrived, but at that point he was pretty "relaxed," like most of the crowd.

He gave me a hug, complimented me again on my pictures, and then whispered that he needed to get going. Someone was watching his stuff on his bench, and he did not want to be gone too long lest his friend wandered off and somebody stole his belongings.

An hour or so later, as the reception came to an end, my friend Paul and his wife, Caroline, offered to give me a ride home in their new Mercedes. As we drove past Farragut Park and stopped at a light, I looked over at Homer's bench and there he was, back in his normal clothes, slowly taking inventory of the contents of his bags and of his adventure. Homer was home.

Chapter 24

President Donald J. Trump

EYES THAT SPEAK 153

Donald J. Trump | Code Name: Mogul
January 2017-2021

THAT WAS MY SEVENTH U.S. presidential inauguration. It was also the easiest one I had ever covered. Since covering the previous Obama inauguration, I had recuperated from two total knee replacements, and a previously broken spine which earned me a disabled parking pass. Thankfully this permitted me to go through various Humvee security checkpoint barricades, as I made my way to the coveted parking space just outside my destination — the Dirksen Building at the U.S. Capitol. Avoiding the struggle of the metro and hauling all my gear made such a difference from previous inaugurations. The weather was mild and that, too, was a great relief from the traditional bitter cold of previous years. It seemed the crowd got a slow start, but the inauguration was well attended.

Inaugurations are followed by more groups with agendas. The next day, women all over the country came out to protest President Trump being elected. A huge rally was held in Washington, D.C., across the United States and even other countries and became known as "the Pink Revolution." Thousands of women marched in many cities here and abroad, wearing pink hats in solidarity. Weeks before the election, Trump had been accused of sexually violating more than 16 women. That was followed by public outrage stemming from an audio clip of a conversation where he admittedly bragged about grabbing women by their private parts and getting away with it because of his fame.

continued on page 158

Left: President Trump is sworn in as the 45th president; the new first lady, Melania Trump, is escorted to the inauguration.

Chapter 24 | President Donald J. Trump

*Early morning of Trump's inauguration.
Below: Later in the day, the crowds have grown.*

Former U.S. Secretary of State and Senator from Massachusetts John Kerry amid the Women's March crowd.

EYES THAT SPEAK 157

Chapter 24 | President Donald J. Trump

Since the change to the Trump administration, there had been a lot of chaos. After four years, and lots of tweeting storms from the president himself, the members of the Press Corps had become public enemy number one to him, and he would continue to let everyone know that. The face of news had been forever changed. It seemed that the new normal was that a significant amount of reporting seemed to be about espousing opinion.

The public decided who they agreed with and that was where they went for their news source. Gone were the days of just straight fact reporting. At the Trump White House, social media became the way the president communicated. Through tweeting, President Trump seemed to be reporting on himself. His use of Twitter was his way of bypassing others' interpretative reporting of his opinions and comments. The president had been quoted as saying, "When somebody challenges you, fight back. Be brutal, be tough."

On a more personal level, not since the Kennedys had there been such an involvement of family. Trump's daughter Ivanka held the title of assistant to the president, and her husband, Jared Kushner, was a senior advisor. Both had become vital members of the president's team with access to the Oval Office and

158 EYES THAT SPEAK

the entire West Wing. We even saw their small children occasionally when the family traveled.

First lady Melania captivated the world with her beauty and sense of fashion when she first arrived at the White House. Her initiative, Be Best, can be summed up by the first lady's own words: "It remains our generation's moral imperative to take responsibility and help our children manage the many issues they are facing today, including encouraging positive social, emotional and physical habits." During the course of her position as first lady, I did not cover many events as with previous first ladies.

The Trump White House demanded that the media be there three to four days a week in order to preserve our precious hard pass. That meant that members of the Press Corps had to be on the White House grounds on days when the president was

continued on page 162

Top: The president announces the Congressional Tax Reduction Package, his first and largest legislative victory in 2017.

Opposite: President Trump often would stop to take questions from the media on his way to boarding Marine One on the South Lawn of the White House.

Chapter 24 | President Donald J. Trump

From top left (clockwise): First lady Melania looks on; President Trump, first lady and son Barron; the Kushner family arrive on the South Lawn; Ivanka and Jared Kushner enter the East Room.

Grandfather Trump escorts grandchildren Arabella and Joseph to Marine One.

Not since the Kennedys had there been such an involvement of family.

Above: The president and first lady board Marine One. Right: President Putin's previous visit to the White House in January 2000. Bottom: Prime Minister Netanyahu participates in a two and two presser in February 2017.

not even there. Although daily briefings were discontinued from the press secretary for long periods of time, Cabinet members or high-level members of the president's team would sometimes hold a briefing. Respected Washington Post reporter Dana Milbank wrote an article about that after losing his hard pass of many years: "The White House is drastically curtailing access for all journalists. Briefings have been abolished in favor of unscheduled 'gaggles' (on the record, but impromptu and haphazard) in the White House driveway." The White House was thinning out the herd, and all of us lived in fear of losing our passes.

In less anxious times, we that work the White House beat covered the president as he invited heads of state or dignitaries from around the world, most of the time for a working visit. Sometimes a two and two press conference would be held, often featuring questions about the latest drama at the White House.

More chaos ensued when President Trump fired former FBI Director James Comey on May 9, 2017. One month later, Comey testified before the Senate Intelligence Committee on what had transpired between him and the president in at least two private meetings at the White House. Throughout my career, I have covered many hearings on Capitol Hill, and usually the witness arrives loaded up with paperwork — not so with Comey. He arrived empty-handed.

Turmoil continued to follow the president into his second year in office. Speaker of the House Nancy Pelosi stepped into office with her boxing gloves on. Pelosi and Trump engaged in a power struggle over immigration and the border wall he was proposing to build. Things heated up so much that the 2019

President Trump scolds CNN reporter Jim Acosta during a press conference.

EYES THAT SPEAK

Senator John McCain lies in state at the U.S. Capitol.

FBI Director James Comey swears in.

EYES THAT SPEAK 165

Chapter 24 | President Donald J. Trump

Speaker Nancy Pelosi extends a hand to President Trump.

State of the Union (SOTU) address was postponed. The moment was tense as President Trump reached out for the traditional handshake with the Speaker of the House at the start of the address.

Later in his speech, Trump graciously welcomed the newly-elected women of Congress. That was the largest number of women to be elected to Congress in history. Making a solidarity statement, they all dressed in white; Nancy Pelosi clearly in command.

Nine days later, President Trump emerged from the Oval Office, entering the "boxing ring" to announce that he was declaring a national emergency in order to gain funding for the border wall. The ongoing conflict between President Trump and Speaker Nancy Pelosi erupted again in a battle of strategy on May 22, 2019, when Pelosi accused Trump of being involved in an alleged cover-up just before she and Senator Chuck Schumer were to meet with him. Trump responded by not only walking out of the meeting, but having his staff instruct all media on site to immediately relocate to the Rose Garden. His action

Newly elected members of Congress celebrate their victories.

EYES THAT SPEAK 167

Chapter 24 | President Donald J. Trump

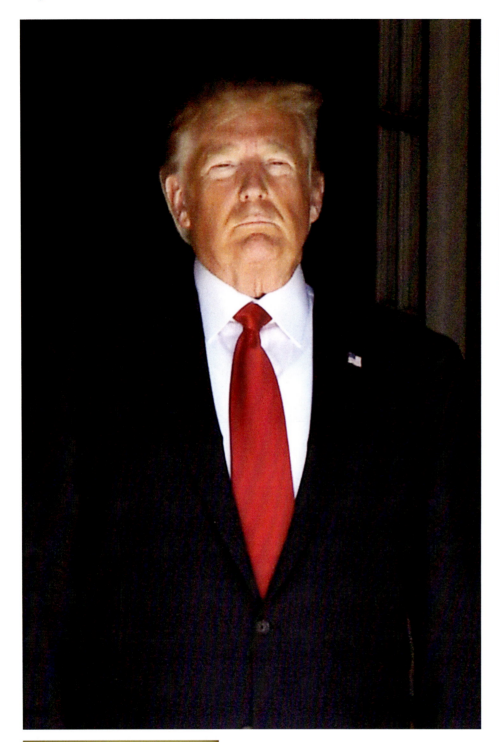

July 15, 2019, President Trump stands in the doorway of the White House as he is being introduced at the Made in America event, celebrating products that are manufactured here in the U.S.
Above: Kellyanne Conway gives the official White House reaction to the proceedings.
Below: Michael Cohen testifies before the Senate.

dominated that round, depriving Pelosi and Schumer of their normal, full media coverage outside the West Wing.

On Feb. 27, 2019, the president's own personal attorney Michael Cohen (known as "the fixer") testified in a controversial hearing before Congress. He disclosed specific, private details about his long, close, working relationship with President Trump just before leaving to serve his prison term.

Then, after almost two years in the making, Special Council Robert Mueller's report was finally released as the first big announcement from newly appointed Attorney General William Barr.

President Trump welcomes World Series Champions Washington Nationals with a bear hug.

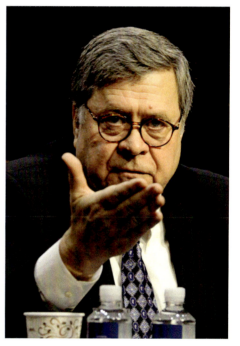

The report investigated Donald Trump for possible collusion with Russia during the 2016 election and other obstruction of justice charges. The report concluded that the Russian government "interfered in the 2016 presidential election in a sweeping and systematic fashion and violated U.S. criminal law."

July 24, 2019, Mueller was subpoenaed by Congress to testify in more detail about his findings.

Two months later, an impeachment inquiry was initiated by Nancy Pelosi, citing Trump had a conversation with Ukrainian president, Volodymyr Zelensky, and withheld funding designated for the

Top left: Former FBI Director Robert Mueller speaks before Congress on July 24, 2019.
Top center: Nancy Pelosi and Chuck Schumer emerge from the West Wing on April 30, 2019.
Top right: Attorney General Barr answers questions from the Senate.

Right: Nov. 15, 2019, the House Intelligence Committee began the second day of the House impeachment hearings.
Above: Nov. 20, 2019, U.S. ambassador to the European Union Gordon Sondland testified before the House Intelligence Committee as his attorney Jim McDermott reacted to Sondland's testimony.

Dec. 18, 2019, President Trump leaves the Oval Office for Christmas vacation as the House of Representatives are meeting to vote on two articles of impeachment against him.

The House managers deliver the articles of impeachment to the Senate Chamber.

Ukraine in exchange for Ukraine investigating presidential candidate Joe Biden and Hunter, his son. The White House pushed back and ignored the subpoenas calling for several people in the Trump administration to testify. Things were never boring at the White House.

On June 30, 2019, President Trump historically traveled to the border of North Korea where he met North Korean leader, Kim Jong Un, and shook hands at the demilitarized zone separating the North and the South. Unfortunately, that big breakthrough turned out to be no more than a photo op.

On Nov. 4, 2019, President Trump welcomed home the Washington Nationals baseball team shortly after they had won the World Series. In a joyful moment, Trump spontaneously gave pitcher Kurt Suzuki a surprise, big bear hug. I was proud to have that image be selected as one of the pictures of the week by the Wall Street Journal.

Nov. 15, 2019, the House Intelligence Committee began the second day of the House impeachment hearings. As

EYES THAT SPEAK 171

Chapter 24 | President Donald J. Trump

Chief Justice John Robers enters the Senate.

former Ukrainian Ambassador Marie Yovanovitch testified, Chairman Adam Schiff received word that President Trump was tweeting about the hearing at that moment.

Jan. 20, 2020, marked the start of the Senate impeachment trial of President Donald J. Trump.

There was silence in hallways of the Capitol as the official procession of the House managers delivered the articles of impeachment to the Senate Chamber. President Donald J. Trump, the 45th president of the United States, was now impeached by the House of Representatives. The charges were Article I, Abuse of Power, and Article 2, Obstruction of Congress. Special passes were then issued to the media to allow access into the Capitol as tensions mounted and security tightened.

U.S. Supreme Court Chief Justice John Roberts presided over the impeachment trial. Each day Justice Roberts would be escorted into the Capitol and through the hallways to the Senate Chambers. Once inside the Chambers, the senators were prohibited by federal law to use cellphones or bring in reading material so they could devote their full attention to all the testimony. I think a few of them were happy to be approached by the flurry of reporters that swarmed them as they exited the Chambers. Since it was an election year, several of the presidential candidates were frustrated because they were stuck hearing impeachment testimony while their competitors were able to continue campaigning all over the country.

As a small news organization, it was very challenging to know where to go because there were so many places to be at one time within the Capitol and, of course, the White House. Many of us crossed paths as we waited outside in the halls, as senators paraded in and out, and then pursued the stakeout locations to get reactions from the senators. As I watched history unfold before me, I was aware that this was my second sitting U.S. president to be impeached. That time, however, I was grateful my position had graduated to being inside the Capitol.

Feb. 4, 2020, just before the final vote from the Senate was decided, the 2020 State of the Union Address took place. That was the most memorable State of the Union Address I have covered.

President Trump greeted Supreme Court Chief Justice Roberts, who was presiding over his impeachment hearings, which had to be an awkward moment for them.

Things got off to a rocky start as President Trump refused to do the traditional handshake with Speaker Pelosi after he gave her a copy of his speech.

Luckily, I happened to have a position near the first lady's box which was where a lot of the action was about to take place. Here were a few of the highlights:

President Trump watched his impeachment hearings closely — sometimes tweeting his comments during the proceedings.

EYES THAT SPEAK 173

Vermont Senator Bernie Sanders held his own as he was surrounded by reporters staking out the internal U.S. Capitol subway.

South Carolina Senator Lindsey Graham

Bottom (left to right): Senators Dick Durbin and Charles Schumer, the House impeachment managers led by Adam Schiff (center) and Utah Senator Mitt Romney who would break from his party to vote for impeachment.

Trump refused the customary handshake with Speaker Pelosi at the 2020 State of the Union.

Greeting Supreme Court Chief Justice Roberts at the State of the Union, which had to be awkward for the two. Roberts was presiding over the impeachment trial.

State of the Union 2020
Top Left: Venezuelan opposition leader Juan Guaidó.
Left: Tuskegee Airman, Brig. General Charles McGee.
Above: Rush Limbaugh receives the Presidential Medal of Freedom from the first lady.

President Trump showed his strong support for Venezuelan opposition leader Juan Guaidó, as he suddenly stepped out of the shadows and waved to the audience from the first lady's box. President Trump then honored 100-year-old Tuskegee Airman, Brig. General Charles McGee (who was just newly promoted). Moments later Trump called out radio talk show host Rush Limbaugh, who was recently diagnosed with stage four lung cancer, and announced that he was about to receive the Presidential Medal of Freedom. Limbaugh seemed as stunned as the rest of us as the first lady turned to present him with the honor.

At the end of the evening, Speaker Pelosi tore up her copy of President Trump's remarks at the end of his speech in retaliation and holding true to their ongoing conflict. Unfortunately, I had left the House Chamber moments earlier and did not capture that moment.

Feb. 5, 2020, Senate Majority Leader Mitch McConnell walked to the Senate Chamber for the final impeachment trial vote. A group of us waited outside the Senate Chamber doors as we all stood listening to the votes being called out. I witnessed history again as Supreme Court Justice John Roberts left the Senate Chamber after the vote was completed, acquitting President Trump. The votes were 48-52 for Abuse of Power and 47-53 on Obstruction of Congress.

Feb. 6, 2020, we rushed down to the White House to an open press access event in the East Room, where President Trump was to make a statement about his acquittal. I was so grateful to be in the overpacked room as the president thanked his supporters and proudly held

Top: Senate Majority Leader Mitch McConnell
Right: Supreme Court Justice John Roberts leaving the Senate after the vote to acquit.

up the front page of the Washington Post declaring his acquittal. I felt I had come full circle in my career as I captured a second sitting U.S. president responding to the final decision of his impeachment hearings.

On March 13, 2020, after all the impeachment drama, things had appeared to calm down when President Trump declared a national state of emergency as the world began the battle against the COVID-19 pandemic. The president held almost daily briefings with his coronavirus task force headed by Vice President Mike Pence and his team of world-class doctors led by infectious disease specialist, Dr. Anthony Fauci. They updated the nation and announced new findings and strategies in dealing with the deadly virus. On most days, they also announced the latest death toll, both in the U.S. and globally, while attempting to keep our country calm but safe from further spreading of the virus. Many felt that the president was taking that as an opportunity to campaign a bit for re-election while he had everyone's attention as he reviewed some of his accomplishments while serving as president.

May 25, 2020, George Floyd, an African American man, died on Memorial Day after he was held down while in handcuffs with the knee of a white Minnesota police officer on his neck for almost nine minutes. His death was recorded on a bystander's cellphone, posted to social media and then picked up by the major networks. A short time later, the public

EYES THAT SPEAK 177

Chapter 24 | President Donald J. Trump

I felt I had come full circle in my career as I captured a second sitting U.S. president responding to the final decision of his impeachment hearings.

Top: Feb. 6, 2020, President Trump displays that morning's Washington Post announcing his acquittal.

Left: President Trump and Vice President Pence leave the Oval Office to announce a national state of emergency due to the COVID-19 pandemic.

Below: Dr. Deborah Brix and the other members of the White House coronavirus task force lay out their plan for battling the virus.

exploded in outrage resulting in demonstrations and riots that rippled across the country and then globally for almost two weeks. The Floyd murder followed several other recent killings of Black people by white police officers in just a few months' time, bringing the ongoing problems of racism and police reform into the spotlight once again.

I need to say that I have worked alongside many professional and kind officers in my career whether on Capitol Hill, at the White House or elsewhere. I believe that the confidence people have in law enforcement is at risk. Officers that are taking the law into their own hands and abusing their position need to be identified and held accountable.

A nearly emptied Washington struggles with the coronavirus pandemic.

Left: A minister stands outside of St. John's Church looking out over protesters who are chanting George Floyd's last words, "I can't breathe."

Bottom: St. John's Church is boarded up after being vandalized and set on fire the night before. A Bible with a note attached reading "BLM" — Black Lives Matter — sits at the door of the church.

Covering this important part of history during the middle of a pandemic was tricky for those of us in the media, risking our own personal safety, not only from demonstrators, but also from exposure to the COVID-19 virus. Most of the protesters in Washington, D.C., during the Black Lives Matter demonstrations, did wear masks and there was not as much violence as in other cities across the country. However, there was unnecessary rioting and looting, and curfews had to be put in place. One week later, across from the White House, President Trump had peaceful protesters forcibly removed via tear gas and rubber bullets from near St. John's Church (known as the "Church of the

EYES THAT SPEAK 181

Chapter 24 | President Donald J. Trump

Top: Protesters are kept out of Lafayette Park by Washington, D.C., police, Homeland Security agents and even the military as they continue to demonstrate as close as they can get to the White House.

Left: The White House brought in police and security personnel from a variety of DOJ sources, including the Dept. of Homeland Security.

President") to clear his path so that he could participate in a photo op there with some of his staff. He did not make any remarks but stood holding a Bible upside down for a couple of minutes as a few of his staff stood uncomfortably, posing for pictures at the president's request. Needless to say, this enraged many folks on a lot of levels.

Oct. 4, 2020, President Trump was hospitalized at Walter Reed Hospital for treatment of COVID-19. During his three days of treatment there, many of his followers showed up to offer their support.

Upon being released, President Trump hit the ground running as he continued to hold campaign rallies across the country, sometimes three in one day. He held many rallies in airport hangers, with Air Force One as the backdrop, while continuing to demonize the media during his remarks.

Following the presidential election, results showed Joe Biden to have won the race, making him the 46th president of the United States. President Trump

Top: Protesters on the streets of Washington, D.C.

Right: Vandalism across the Washington area included tagging many buildings, including the White House Historical Association.

had refused to accept the election, citing widespread electoral fraud, and he vowed to fight the election results in court. The president went on camera stating, "The only way they can take this election away from us is if this is a rigged election. We're going to win this election."

For several weeks prior to the Biden inauguration, President Trump's normally itemized daily schedule simply read: "President Trump will work from early in the morning until late in the evening. He will make many calls and have many meetings."

With the 2021 inauguration just a couple of weeks away, Trump remained mostly out of the public eye as he figured out his next move while the world watched.

President Trump made his final public appearance as president when he took the stage on Jan. 6 at a Save America Rally on the Ellipse.

Chapter 25

Insurrection
at the U.S. Capitol

The crowd makes its way up Pennsylvania Avenue toward the U.S. Capitol

Capitol Hill
Jan. 6, 2021

Chapter 25 | Insurrection

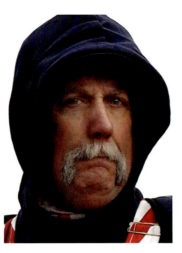

PRESIDENT TRUMP WAS SCHEDULED to speak at a rally on the Ellipse across from the White House on Jan. 6. It was rumored that he was going to encourage his supporters to march to the U.S. Capitol to protest the presidential election results as Congress was gathered there to count the Electoral College ballots. That was the process where the votes from the 2020 election from each state were formally calculated. All members of Congress would be there. Vice President Pence would preside.

I had hoped to get some pictures inside the Senate Chamber, one of the rare times photographers were allowed, but I was denied access due to COVID-19 restrictions. Over the course of several days, busloads of Trump supporters continued arriving in Washington, D.C., and locals around the Washington area were warned via radio and TV to avoid going downtown on Jan. 6. Businesses were closing down and boarding up their storefronts in anticipation of trouble. I decided to stake out the U.S. Capitol.

I reasoned that being imbedded in the crowd at the Trump Rally would have me somewhat pinned in, and I felt it would be a better vantage point to be at the destination of where the crowd was most likely headed.

The large group of folks where I was, on the east side of the Capitol, were mostly older white people, many veterans who attentively listened on their cellphones to President Trump's live remarks taking place just down the street. Hundreds of the Trump supporters had their cellphones on speaker so they could listen to his speech creating an amplified symphony effect to his voice throughout the growing crowd.

"We fight like hell. And if you don't fight like hell, you're not going to have a country anymore." He then said to his audience, "We have hundreds of thousands of people here and I just want them to be

Protestors dress to express their political opinions at the Capitol on Jan. 6.

recognized by the fake news media. The media is the biggest problem we have as far as I'm concerned, single biggest problem. The fake news and the big tech."

Vice President Pence arrived at the Capitol toward the end of President Trump's rally, followed by a growing stream of protesters that appeared to be a bit more hardcore and anxious — the vibe was quickly changing.

I looked down and saw that I had lost my cellphone! I had thought it was gone for good but with the help of two friends, I was able to track down the former Vietnam veteran who had found my phone and returned it to me in the middle of all the chaos — refusing a reward. Such a kind soul in the middle of the growing tension.

Out on Constitution Avenue, a large mass of protesters could be seen approaching from Pennsylvania Avenue a few blocks away. Several Capitol Police near me appeared anxious as they looked at the size of the crowd steadily heading our way.

As I turned, I found myself face-to-face with a few dozen of the Proud Boys. Many of them had walkie-talkies. As they marched with an air of authority toward me, I continued to fire away, taking

Vice President Pence arrives at the Capitol shortly before the end of Trump's speech.

EYES THAT SPEAK **187**

The Proud Boys arrive at the U.S. Capitol equipped with walkie-talkies to communicate with each other.

Chapter 25 | Insurrection

Crowds gathering at the Capitol.

pictures. One of them began shouting "F--- the media!" as if it were a battle cry. I knew then that it was time to stash my credentials under my jacket and I slid behind a tree to do that. Others could be heard shouting "CNN sucks" and that the media reported fake news and could not be trusted. Members of the press were threatened, punched and cameras were smashed. It seemed that the media had really become the enemy of the people, as President Trump had claimed throughout his term in office. A member of a TV news crew even had their camera and gear lit on fire on the west side of the Capitol.

A man near me warned an older woman that his group was about to break down the riot fencing and that she should get out of the way so she would not get trampled. Suddenly, the crowd began shouting, "Stop The Steal!" He pointed to the fencing 20 yards away as more police arrived in riot gear in an attempt to hold the swelling crowd back. A large mass of people from the Trump rally began to arrive just as the crowd around me began to knock down the protective fencing that held the protesters back. The two groups then merged and marched to the steps of the Capitol.

Police tried to keep them from going up the steps, but they were vastly outnumbered and were forced to retreat out of sight. The Capitol Police did the best

Fences are broken down as the crowd from the rally merged with those protesting outside the Capitol.

they could, since they were not given the proper protective gear or additional manpower that they were desperately requesting for hours.

In the meantime, on the west side of the Capitol, gallows were being built, complete with nooses.

Hundreds of people rushed up the stairs to the doors of the Capitol while shouting and chanting, "Hang Mike Pence! Hang Mike Pence!"

I paced myself with the crowd as we moved to the steps of the Capitol, and I could feel the people beginning to surge, so I made my way to the outer side of the crowd. That way I would not be pinned in and unable to take pictures of anything other than the back of the heads of the people in front of me. I then became aware that the protesters were quickly closing in all around me. I was swept up in a sea of moving people that were quickly becoming a mob. The crowd reached the top of the stairs and began banging on the doors and windows, finally breaking through the glass. Heading over to the west front of the Capitol, things were getting more violent and tear gas canisters and flash bombs were being deployed both by the protesters and, later, police. I had no protective gear and so was forced to retreat. We noticed a rescue squad trying to make its way through the crowd. They were responding to a call that one protester had been shot in the neck. She died at the

Chapter 25 | Insurrection

Protestors gather on the Capitol grounds, including members of the Proud Boys, following President Trump's speech. Some of the protesters came prepared with gas masks and various weapons.

scene. Over one hundred Capitol police officers were injured that day and several members of the media were threatened both physically and verbally.

Members of Congress were told to remove their pins that identified them, then were evacuated from the Chamber and taken to a secure area and ordered to "shelter in place." A total of five people were killed due to the insurrection at the Capitol.

The vice president, while being escorted to a secure location, came within several yards of the intruders. Once inside the building, the rioters began banging on doors and trying to break through the locks of office doors before finally gaining access to the Chamber floor itself, where moments earlier Vice President Mike Pence had stood.

Capitol Police retreat as they are rushed by a crowd of thousands who were chanting "Hang Mike Pence." Soon they made it up the stairs and to the door of the Capitol, where they were pounding on the door and breaking windows to enter the building.

The crowd proclaims victory from the balcony of the Capitol.

A view of the Statue of Freedom atop the U.S. Capitol as seen through the riot fencing and razor wire.

Chapter 26
President Joseph R. Biden

Due to COVID-19, the Biden inauguration had limited attendees and featured — for the first time — a virtual format, with limited participants, televised for the public to view safely.

Joseph R. Biden | Code Name: Celtic
January 2021-Present

Instead of the traditional crowd of citizens, the Biden inaguration had 25,000 armed National Guard surrounding the Capitol.

MY EIGHTH U.S. PRESIDENTIAL INAUGURATION was like no other. There were a limited number of photographic positions for the Biden inauguration and, unfortunately, I was dealt a terrible spot.

I ended up with a worse spot than the triangle position I had on my first Clinton inauguration. From my vantage point, I was visually blocked by the podium and unable to capture Kamala Harris, the first African American and Asian American woman to be sworn in as vice president of the United States. Once again, finding myself coming full circle, I was disappointed but grateful to be on the Capitol grounds at all for that historic event. I guess I will only have those images I witnessed in my memory. The COVID-19 pandemic rules had dictated that a very limited number of photographers were allowed to be present for the ceremony. Almost everything was done virtually.

One week earlier, President Trump had been impeached for the second time by the House of Representatives, charging him with Incitement of Insurrection based on the events that took place on Jan. 6 at the Capitol. He was then once again acquitted by the Senate.

Following the insurrection, President Trump had his Twitter account suspended indefinitely, cutting off his main form of communication. Trump has remained a powerful influence within the Republican Party, and it remains to be seen what his next move will be in the upcoming future.

Chapter 26 | President Joseph R. Biden

Clockwise from below, left: Newly elected Vice President Kamala Harris waves at the cameras from behind the bulletproof glass; members of the National Guard wait outside the Capitol grounds during the ceremony; Lady Gaga performs "The Star-Spangled Banner"; President Biden is congratulated by his son Hunter following his swearing in; Joseph R. Biden swears in as the 46th president of the United States; former President Trump flies over the U.S. Capitol for the final time as 45th president of the United States as workers were preparing for the Biden Inaugural ceremony.

President Trump chose not to attend the Biden inauguration. A couple of hours prior to the ceremony, he did a flyover on Marine One for the final time over the U.S. Capitol on the way to his own departure ceremony at Joint Base Andrews.

Meanwhile, the inaugural ceremonies featured performers Lady Gaga, J.Lo and Garth Brooks, and 22-year-old Amanda Gorman made her debut as the youngest inaugural poet in history, as she read her wonderful original poem, "The Hill We Climb."

I felt that during the exchange of power this time, there was a sense of exhaling after all that had been going on for the prior months and longer.

While watching the ceremonial celebration at the Capitol, we members of the media recalled that two weeks earlier in the same place, a deadly insurrection at the U.S. Capitol had taken place. Those of us inside the buffer zone were now surrounded by a nine-foot riot fencing complete with razor wire, and 25,000 National Guard troops — far outnumbering those of us that were

attendees at the inaugural ceremony itself.

The year of 2020 had been surreal and 2021 began with the return of more mass shootings across the country, an increase in hate crimes, unresolved immigration issues and many other ongoing problems that have yet to be solved, yet somehow there seems to be a glimmer of hope in the air.

It is in times like these, I am reminded of my old friend and bureau chief Sarah McClendon's words from long ago:

"Be sure to always keep an eye on the president ... "

Author's Biography

BEFORE SHE JUMPED out of an airplane at 15,000 feet and earned her first-degree black belt in Tae Kwon Do, Christy Bowe, a third-generation Washingtonian, was thrown out of Catholic school in the ninth grade for refusing to conform. She briefly attended Montgomery College of Rockville, Maryland, and the University of Missouri Photo Workshop in Carthage, Missouri.

Most of her education has been "on the job."

In pursuit of her passion for photography, Christy earned her way into the small, elite circle of White House press photographers. With support from celebrated White House reporter, the late Sarah McClendon, Christy started ImageCatcher News Service. She is represented by Getty Images, Zuma Press and Polaris Images.

Her pictures have been featured in magazines such as Time, Newsweek, Vanity Fair, and Rolling Stone. Christy has been published by Wadsworth Publishing and McGraw-Hill, and the autobiography of retired U.S. Supreme Court Justice John Paul Stevens — "The Making of a Justice."

Her corporate clients have included: Harley Davidson, the National Science Foundation, the National Press Club, the National Organization for Women and Hitachi Corporation.

Christy is currently a member of the White House Press Corps, House and Senate Press Photographers' Gallery, White House Correspondents' Association and White House News Photographers' Association. She has lectured at American University, Montgomery College and George Mason University among others. She has ten images preserved in the George W. Bush Presidential Library and won first place in the 2021 Paris Photo Prize — the State of the World competition for her pictures of the January 6 insurrection. Christy resides in Bethesda, Maryland, and continues to work as a photojournalist, currently covering her fifth U.S. president, Joseph R. Biden.

From left to right: Former Secretary of State Madeleine Albright, author Christy Bowe, Helen Thomas, Christiane Amanpour in 2008

Author Christy Bowe with ERT Secret Service Agent Barry Donadio.